The Museum Guide to Dorking

a brief history of the town and surrounding villages

by

Kathy Atherton

Published by The Cockerel Press

British Library Cataloguing in Publication Data

Atherton, Kathy
The Museum Guide to Dorking: a brief history of the town and surrounding villages
ISBN 978-1-909871-00-7

All proceeds of the sale of this publication will go to Dorking Museum & Heritage Centre, 62 West Street, Dorking, Surrey RH4 1BS
www.dorkingmuseum.org.uk

A large number of people have had input into this book and into the museum panels on which this book is based.
Thanks for initial research must go to Hannah Flowerday, Susannah Horne, and Bette Phillips. Comment, criticism and advice on early drafts was provided by Tom Fedrick (prehistory), Professor Richard Selley (geology and caves), Frank Pemberton (archaeology), Heather and Fergus Cannan-Braniff (editorial), Mary Day (early settlement, industry and John Beckett), Martin Cole (Brockham Park, railways), Tom Loftus (Johnstons, railways), Chris and Michele Kohler (Darwin and Leith Hill Place), Sandra Wedgwood (the Wedgwoods), Renee Stewart (the Leith Hill Musical Festival), Allan Brigham (town development) and Vivien Ettlinger (early settlement and William Mullins).
Neither panels nor book could have been produced without the help of Dorking Museum & Heritage Centre archives run by Jane le Cluse and Bobbie Rounthwaite and the team who ferreted out all the images and documents, in particular Isabel McClennan, Sarah Brogden, Donna Pilcher, Pat Womersley, and Virginia Wheeler.
Clare Flanagan provided invaluable picture research; Roy Williamson took the artefact pictures and Julie Goodliffe provided information on the artefacts. Sue Tombs, Lauren Kyle and Lisa Geelhood undertook the proofreading. Peter Camp and Lorraine Spindler provided editorial and production advice.

THE
COCKEREL
PRESS

Introduction

Welcome to your virtual tour of Dorking Museum. Like the panels from which it is derived, this book does not seek to provide a comprehensive history of the town, its surrounding countryside and villages, in conventional chapters. Rather, it explores events, themes and individuals which have played a part in the town's history in an impressionistic way, enabling the reader to dip in and out.

For the visitor to the Museum, we hope that it will prove an enhancement to the experience, allowing for later reflection. For those unable to visit, it offers an alternative experience.

Covering a wider geographical area than the traditional manor and parish of Dorking, the book encompasses the countryside and villages for which Dorking has long been a focus of economic activity, trade and culture: from Brockham and Betchworth in the east to Wotton and Abinger in the west, and from Box Hill and Mickleham in the north to Capel, Ockley and Newdigate in the south.

Your tour will take you from the formation of the chalk of Box Hill 120 million years ago, (and the fearsome creatures that inhabited the area then), to the groundbreaking development of semi- synthetic penicillins in the 20th century, by way of some surprises: Pilgrim Fathers, riots, suffragettes, and pioneering industries.

Enjoy the journey!

Top: The Gun Inn, North Street by GM Downing
Middle: The White Horse, High (East) Street by Charles Collins
Bottom: The Spotted Dog, South Street by George Gardiner
With the coming of the turnpike road in 1755, Dorking became a coaching stop on the east-west and north-south roads with the result that inns proliferated. All images: Dorking Museum

Why is Dorking where it is?

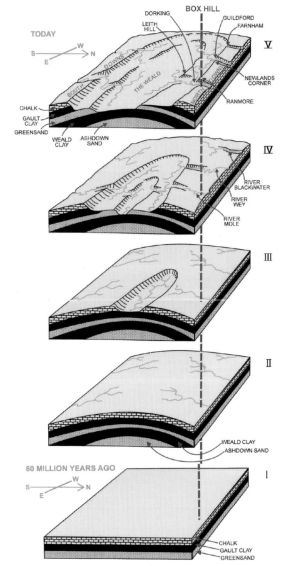

Dorking lies where the River Mole cuts a gap in the hard chalk ridge of the North Downs.

This 'Mole gap' separates Ranmore Common in the west from Box Hill in the east, creating a travel route through to the north. This is the point where today both the A24 and the London-bound railway cross the North Downs.

Geology is responsible for the distinctive countryside that surrounds Dorking, for its position, and for the positions of the surrounding villages. It has played a significant role in the town's history.

The town and nearby villages have benefited from the area's abundant natural supplies of water, sand, chalk, clay and timber. Today Dorking and the surrounding countryside attract hundreds of thousands of visitors every year. But for centuries Dorking and its satellite villages remained isolated and impoverished.

The landscape was created by geological forces. 60 million years ago movement in the earth's crust forced the layers under southern England to dome upwards. Erosion of the top layers of chalk exposed the geological layers below, leaving the North and South Downs chalk ridges, the hard sandstone outcrops of Leith Hill, Holmbury Hill and the Nower, and a large area of exposed Weald clay to the south.

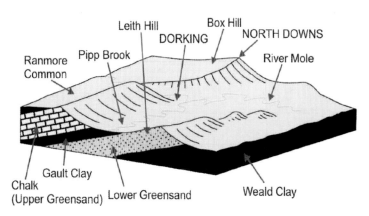

At the foot of the North Downs chalk ridge of Box Hill and Ranmore, the Mole flows over Gault clay towards the town. At Pixham it converges with the Pipp Brook to flow north. Layers of greensand, which lie beneath the clay, crop out around the town. Hard and resistant to weathering, the greensand gives rise to a chain of hills: the Deepdene, the Nower and - at almost 100 metres the highest point in southern England - Leith Hill. To the south is the Weald clay.

Geological diagrams ©The Friends of Box Hill

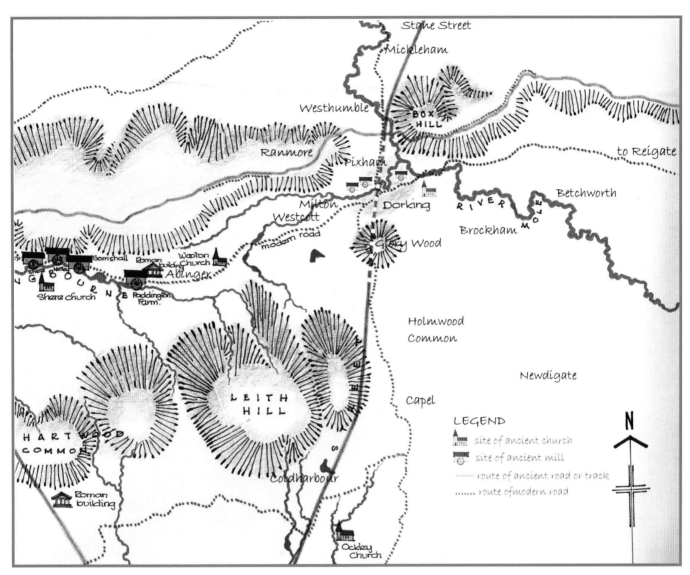

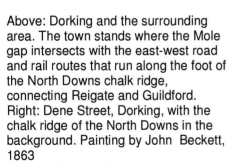

Above: Dorking and the surrounding area. The town stands where the Mole gap intersects with the east-west road and rail routes that run along the foot of the North Downs chalk ridge, connecting Reigate and Guildford.
Right: Dene Street, Dorking, with the chalk ridge of the North Downs in the background. Painting by John Beckett, 1863
Images: Dorking Museum

Cretaceous Dorkinians

The geology of Mole Valley was formed when Earth's climate was warm and sea levels were high.

Between 65 and 100 million years ago

southern England lay under a warm sea. The chalk of the North Downs was formed from the bodies of millions of marine plants and animals that lived there. Spectacular fossil fish, ammonites and sea urchins from this sea have been found in the chalk quarries of Ranmore.

Between 110 and 120 million years ago

migrating underwater sand dunes covered this area in a shallow, sandy sea. They were buried and cemented to form the greensand of the hills to the south of the town.

Over 120 million years ago

northern Europe was covered by lakes, marshes and lagoons. Sediment from the rivers flowing into the lakes from the swampy plain that covered southern England formed the thick Weald Clay that is found to the south of Dorking. The remains of the dinosaurs which roamed the Dorking area have been found in the clays of Capel and Ockley.

The rock layers of Mole Valley

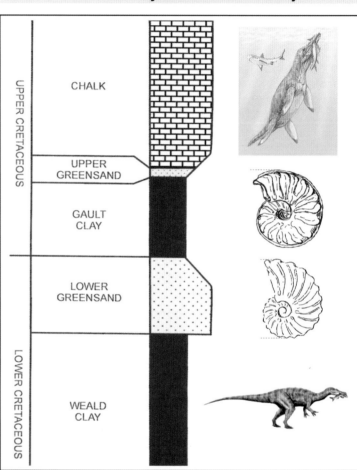

120 to 65 million years ago: oldest layers on the bottom of the diagram.

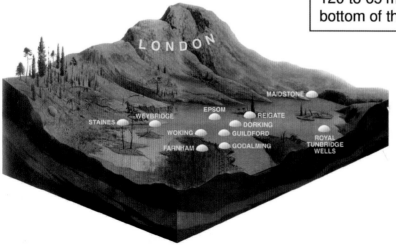

Left: south-east England 130 million years ago (the early Cretaceous period)
Image: Surrey Archaeological Society and Surrey Country Archaeology Unit (part of Surrey County Council)

Baryonyx walkeri

In 1983 amateur fossil hunter William Walker discovered a huge bone at the Smokejack clay pits at Walliswood near Ockley. The previously unknown species was named after its discoverer and the fossilized skeleton is now on display at the Natural History Museum. Known as the 'Surrey Dinosaur' *Baryonyx* had crocodile jaws and was the first fish-eating dinosaur to be discovered.

Baryonyx grew to ten metres long. The name means 'heavy claw' and it was so named because it had a 30 centimetre long claw on each hand.

Iguanodon

A fossilized *Iguanodon* metres down during well shaft in the clay at Capel in 1891. found at Redlands, *Iguanodon* was one of successful dinosaurs.

tail was found 30 the digging of a Broomells Farm, Another has been South Holmwood. the most

A plant-eater which probably lived in herds, *Iguanodon* was nine to ten metres long with webbed hoof-like fingertips, a large spike on its thumb and a wide beak.

Polyptychodon interruptus

A fossilized skull of this rare fish-eating sea creature was found in the Dorking chalk pits in the 1850s. It was an important find and of great scientific significance, becoming the 'type' fossil for this species.

At the request of Lord Ashcombe of Denbies, the fossil was studied by the great 19th century dinosaur anatomist, Richard Owen - the man who gave the name 'dinosauria' to the great reptiles that he studied. Owen described the specimen at a meeting of the Geological Society in December 1859.

About seven metres long, *Polyptychodon* had a long saw-like jaw and huge eye cavities.

Images above by Jon Hughes and Russell Gooday of Pixel-shack.com reproduced by permission of Quercus Publishing PLC
Right: Polyptychodon by permission of Dmitry Bogdanov

Plesiosaurs and Pterosaurs

Marine and flying reptiles from the Lower Chalk near Dorking

Marine reptiles named plesiosaurs lived in the seas around Dorking in the late Cretaceous period. Plesiosaurs became extinct at the end of the Cretaceous period. Lord Ashcombe collected fossils of two types of plesiosaur in the area: pliosaurs and elasmosaurs.

Liopleurodon, a type of pliosaur

Pliosaurs had fins, a large head and a short neck and tail. The tail was not used for propulsion. The biggest pliosaurs reached 15 metres in length and would have weighed 45 tonnes. *Polyptychodon* was a type of pliosaur.

Elasmosaurs were similar to pliosaurs but they had extremely long necks - some had over 70 vertebrae (spinal bones) - and small heads.

Elasmosaurus, a type of elasmosaur

The local chalk pits have also yielded up fossils of the huge flying reptiles that took to the skies around Dorking.

Pterodactylus, a type of pterosaur

The *Pterodactylus* was a type of pterosaur. Its name means 'winged finger'. A flying reptile, it had extended wrist bones and the wing skin was attached to its long 4th finger. It may have had fur or primitive feathers.
The fish-eating *Pterodactylus* hunted in the seas that covered the Dorking and Ranmore area in the Cretaceous period.

Images reproduced by permission of Nobu Tamura

Life Under the Sea

The Cretaceous seas that formed the chalk of Box Hill and Ranmore teemed with life. The remains of turtles and sharks, sea urchins, sponges and starfish have been found preserved in local rocks.

Many species, such as the fishes *Xiphactinus* and *Ctenothrissa,* which lived in the sea that covered the Dorking area in the Cretaceous period, are now extinct.

Xiphactinus (right) was a predatory bony fish that could reach 6 metres in length.

Ptychodus deccurrens was a shell-crushing shark, also now extinct. Its rows of crushing and grinding teeth were arranged top and bottom like a pavement, enabling it to crush the shells of clams and other prey.

Above: *Ptychodus mortoni*, closely related to the *Ptychodus deccurrens*
Left and below: fossil mollusc, ammonite and fish from Lord Ashcombe's collection
Images reproduced by permission of Dmitri Bogdanov

Lord Ashcombe's Teeth

George Cubitt, 1st Baron Ashcombe.
When he announced his intention of marrying Laura Joyce, daughter of the vicar of Dorking, his self-made millionaire father threatened disinheritance.

George Cubitt MP, son of the master builder Thomas Cubitt, inherited the Denbies estate in 1855. In 1892 he became Baron Ashcombe of Dorking and Bodiam Castle, taking the name from Ashcombe Wood.

Lord Ashcombe assembled an important geological collection at Denbies. Many of his pieces were unearthed during chalk quarrying at Ranmore. He rewarded employees for delivering fossils to him and shared his discoveries with early experts. His *Iguanodon* tail is displayed at Dorking Museum in the case which he had built to display it in the hallway at Denbies.

George Cubitt's fossils were given to the Museum in 1948 by his grandson, Roland, the 3rd Baron Ashcombe. They are fondly known as 'Lord Ashcombe's teeth'.

Chalk quarrying at Dorking lime works (now the household waste site) in about 1910. Image: Dorking Museum

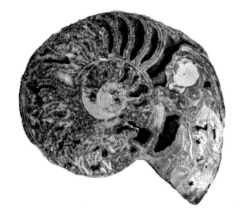

Above: An ammonite from the collection of Lord Ashcombe which has been sectioned to show the body parts. It was not locally sourced. The ammonite was a cephalopod mollusc which swam backwards. Its closest living relation is the nautilus which is related to the octopus. Ammonites became extinct at the end of Cretaceous period along with the dinosaurs. Artist's impression of an ammonite reproduced by permission of Nobu Tamura

Mole Valley Mammals of the Ice Age

During the Ice Age, two and a half million to 12,000 years ago, sea levels fell as water was locked up in the glaciers that covered much of the Northern Hemisphere. The River Mole deposited gravel as it meandered across its flood plain. Fossilized remains of the large mammals ('Megafauna') that roamed the area have been found in these gravels.

The Great Auroch

Fossilized molars (teeth) and leg bones of a great auroch (*Bos primigenius)* were found not far from the Pixham/A24 roundabout.
The auroch is the ancestor of modern cattle. These cattle were enormous by today's standards; two metres tall, they weighed a ton.

Woolly Rhinoceros

Fossilized molars (teeth) and bones of a woolly rhinoceros *(Coelodonta antiquitatis* meaning 'cavity tooth') were also found not far from the Pixham/A24 roundabout.
The woolly rhino was about four metres long and two metres tall. Weighing two and a half tons it had two horns, one of which could reach a metre in length.

Woolly Mammoth

Huge molars (teeth) from a woolly mammoth (*Mammuthus primigenius*), and a femur (leg bone), were found in the same area. A male mammoth could grow up to four metres tall and had winter hair a metre long. Its curved tusks could reach five metres in length. The mammoth was adapted for a cold climate: its ears were small to prevent heat loss; its skin contained grease-producing cells for insulation; it had a fatty lump on its head for energy storage and a shaggy coat.

Auroch image: Charles Hamilton Smith
Rhino and mammoth images: Mauricio Anton
copyright 2008 Public Library of Science
C..Sedwick 'What killed the woolly mammoth?'
PLoS Biology 6 (4):e99

First Human Residents

At the end of the Ice Age, oak forest spread across much of Sussex and Kent to the chalk ridge of the North Downs.

During the Mesolithic period (c.6,500-4,000 BC) small groups of humans settled across the sandy (greensand) hills to the south of Dorking, living by foraging for fruit and nuts and hunting for fish and game.

Over time they began to cultivate plants and to domesticate animals. The light, well-drained soil of the greensand is easier to work than the heavy clay to the south, and so farming was established between Betchworth and Abinger at the foot of the chalk ridges and along the banks of the Mole.

Round-houses & Hill-forts

By the Bronze Age, roughly 2,500-800 BC, there were burial mounds on the hills at Glory Wood and Milton Heath. High status people were buried on these hills, at the boundaries between local tribes.

Iron Age (800BC-43AD) man built forts at Anstiebury and Holmbury on the greensand hills in the 1st century BC. Their large earthworks would have required considerable man-power. The forts were probably built by farmers who lived in nearby round-houses, such as the one at Mickleham Downs.

Above: artist's impression of a temporary camp made by Mesolithic hunters like those who left their arrow heads and axes around the greensand of Leith Hill. Below: round-house settlement showing how the Iron Age ones at Mickleham Downs may have looked. Image: Surrey Archaeological Society and Surrey County Archaeology Unit (part of Surrey County Council)

Stoney-street

The Romans were the first people to exploit the Mole Gap as a travel route.

The road that they built to bring supplies up from Chichester (Noviomagus) over the Thames at London was later known as 'Stoney-street' because of its flint surface.

Local flints and stones were used to build the road's cambered surface. The road kept to rising ground to avoid the worst of the Weald clay. Its route through Dorking is not precisely known.

There was a Roman settlement in Dorking, concentrated around the St Martin's and High Street area. There was also a Roman villa, with mosaic floors, at Abinger (near Crossways Farm).

When the Roman economy collapsed in the 5th century the road probably fell into disrepair. It was more than 1,000 years before there was another viable road across the Weald to Dorking.

Dorchinges

After the Roman collapse the local population saw a migration of Anglo-Saxon people from the Low Countries into the area.

From the small settlement at Dorking swine herdsmen ran pigs, which fed on beech mast and acorns, in the Wealden woodland to the south. A seasonal herdsmen's settlement grew up at Ewekene (Capel), which in time became a permanent settlement. Between the arable and meadow land close about the settlement and Ewekene the woodland transmuted into a patchwork of scrub, grove and grassland in which the Saxons foraged, took wood and hunted. The long thin 'manor' that evolved, stretching from chalk down through the greensand into the Weald clay is characteristic of the area.

By the time of the Norman Conquest the Saxon manor was known as Dorchinges, which means 'the people of Deorc' in Old English.

Artist's impressions of how Stane Street (above) and a Saxon settlement such as Dorchinges (below) may have looked.
Images: Surrey Archaeological Society and Surrey County Archaeology Unit (part of Surrey County Council)

Dorchinges at Domesday

In 1086 when the king decreed a survey be made of all lands in England, Dorchinges was listed as belonging to the crown.

This survey, called the Domesday Book, reveals that the manor of Dorking had previously been the property of Edith, widow of Edward the Confessor, King of England from 1042-1066.

At the time of Domesday, the manor of Dorking had a church and 3 watermills on the Pipp Brook.
4 serf (landless labourer) families worked the lord of the manor's land to the north of the Pipp Brook, ploughing with teams of 8 oxen. 13 cottager families occupied small plots, working for hire on the lord's lands and grazing pigs on the Cotmandene. 38 families of villeins (who held enough land to support themselves in return for services to the lord) had homes on the tracks leading south from Dorking, on the slopes of Leith Hill and in the Capel clearings.

The landscape around the Manor was a mix of downs, heath, farm and woodland. As the population grew in the centuries after Domesday, land was put to the plough. The lord of the manor of Dorking made grants of land to the east and south of the settlement.

The swine of Dorking and the neighbouring manor settlements were driven down into the Wealden woodland for pannage: fattening on acorns and beech nuts.

Many traditional livelihoods survived until relatively recent times. Above: A shepherd at Hackhurst Farm in around 1900 with coppiced hurdle fencing Below: A hoop-shaver's shelter, Deerleap woods around 1895. Left: A charcoal burner's shelter, Bury Hill estate in about 1910.
All images: Dorking Museum

Agriculture and the 'Wastes'

Life on the land was often hard. The farms to the south of Dorking were cultivated with difficulty. Oxen struggled to plough the clay which was waterlogged in winter and baked hard in summer. To counteract the soil's acidity, marl from lower layers was dug and spread. Yields of wheat, barley, oats or rye were low and when cropped the land needed long periods of rest.

Robert Morden's map (1695) shows 'Darking' with Betchworth Castle (in the neighbouring manor of West Betchworth).

Areas that were not viable for cultivation were known as 'wastes'. These common lands were vital to the local economy. Without access to the wastes tenant farmers would have been unable to survive. So, although the lord hunted on them and harvested them for charcoal, timber, gravel, holly and turf, he granted his tenants 'rights of common' over them – because he relied on his tenants' labour and beasts to cultivate his farm land.

Dorking's largest waste was the 'home' wood, now Holmwood. There were smaller wastes at Beare Green, Misbooks Green, Clarke's Green, Maynack Wood, Ashcombe Heath, Cotmandene, Spital Heath and Mount Heath.

The wastes were vigorously policed. Unauthorized animals were 'impounded' - taken off the commons and put into pounds - with fines payable for their release.

Ploughing with oxen. Image from the 14th century Luttrell Psalter

15

Commoners' Rights

In the medieval period the lordship of the manor of Dorking passed from the Earls de Warenne (who came over with William the Conqueror) and their descendents to the Dukes of Norfolk. The common land was vital to the economy of the manor. For a payment the lord granted rights over commons such as Holmwood, Beare Green and Cotmandene to the manor's tenants.

Piscary was the right to take fish from the manor's streams.

Turbury was the right to take turf or peat from the commons.

Estovers was the right to take fallen wood, 'by hook or by crook' only, for fuel, and to take bracken for animal bedding, which would be spread on the fields for manure in the spring.

Pannage was the right to forage pigs in the lord's coppices such as those at Redlands that provided palings, hurdles, hoops and brooms, and on the wastes.

Herbage was the right to graze grass-eating plough animals on the wastes in the summer months. Herbage was the most important of the rights for which the lord charged his tenants. It was vital to the viability of the manor as if tenant farmers could not grow winter fodder on their own lands but had to graze their animals there during the summer, they would then be unable to over-winter their plough animals and so be unable to plough their land – and that of their lord – in the spring.

Image reproduced by permission of Frances Mountford

Mills and Mill Ponds

In the Domesday survey of 1086 there were three mills in the manor of Dorking. Castle Mill, on the River Mole, is on the site of a Domesday mill. The main block was built in the 18th century, with the wing to the south being added in the 1830s. It was closed in 1952 and is now a private house.

In the 1950s and 1960s it starred in 'the haunted mill' episode of *The Adventures of Robin Hood*, and in two episodes of *The Avengers*.

The Pippbrook, which joins the River Mole below Box Hill, near Pixham Lane, has powered a number of mills: Rookery Mill on the Rookery estate, Westcott Mill, Milton Court Mill, and Parsonage, Pippbrook and Pixham Mills. Pippbook Mill's pond is now part of the Meadowbank recreation ground. Both Parsonage and Pixham Mills were run for decades by the Attlee family of seed merchants and feed suppliers.

At one time the Tillingbourne, which flows west from Leith Hill, had 30 watermills along its length, including those at Friday Street, Broadmoor, Wotton and Abinger. These mills were used not just for corn grinding but also for cloth fulling and gunpowder production.

Pixham Mill at the foot of Box Hill, c1900. Image: Dorking Museum

Castle Mill, Dorking by AC Fare. Image: Dorking Museum

Abinger Mill by Charles Gibbs. Image: Dorking Museum

Pippbrook Mill, Dorking. Image: Dorking Museum

Life in Medieval Dorking

Situated on routes running north to south and east to west, Dorking was a natural trading centre for the surrounding manors and hamlets.

During the Middle Ages a market was held twice a week around the well at Pump Corner in the centre of Dorking. Here smiths, skinners, weavers, tailors, shoemakers and leather workers, bakers, brewers and butchers would congregate to sell their goods and offer their skills. Two inns catered for travelling merchants and artisans: the Cardinal's Hat on East Street (now the High Street) and the George opposite.

Most people made their living on the land. They had to transport wood out of the manor's woods for the markets of Kingston. They needed permission from the lord to marry, to leave the manor and to transfer land. At the lord's open air courts they were sentenced for offences such as throwing refuse into the streets, brewing without a licence, selling underweight bread, felling timber without permission or taking the lord's rabbits.

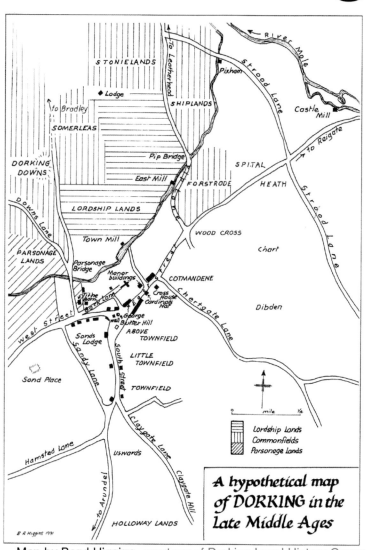

A hypothetical map of DORKING in the Late Middle Ages

Map by Beryl Higgins, courtesy of Dorking Local History Group

Trade tokens inscribed 'Edward Goodwin, of Darking in Surry'

Goodwin made his living as a chandler (a maker or supplier of candles) and this trade token shows a man making candles.
Goodwin was the younger son of the owner of the Queen's Arms on the corner of West Street and North Street. He inherited the inn in 1602.

This fashionable 17th century child's shoe was found placed up a chimney in South Street to ward off spirits. It shows that by the later 17th century Dorking was prosperous enough for some of its residents to be wearing the latest styles.

Isolation and Religion

The remoteness of settlements and the size of local parishes favoured religious non-conformity. The occupants of the outlying villages turned to forms of worship that did not require them to trudge into town but allowed them to establish local meeting houses. A Quaker meeting was established at Kitlands Farm between Coldharbour and Capel in 1655.

Many people in Dorking followed radical, dissenting forms of Protestantism.
In the 1570s Dorking's parish priest, Stephen Richman, was charged with non-conformity. The town was staunchly Parliamentarian during the Civil War and many in town were more radical than Cromwell's government. Violent Fifth Monarchist dissenter Christopher Feake was discovered living in secrecy in Dorking in 1663. At the same time an illegal Independent meeting attracting 100 adherents was being held in Spring Gardens by ousted dissenting minister James Fisher. In the following century Dorking became a centre for Independent Congregational worship and John Wesley made 19 visits to preach, the first in 1764.

These dissenters sometimes found themselves at odds with local business. In the 1670s, the landlord of the King's Arms set up a notorious supper club in a cave near the summit of Box Hill which attracted gentry from Epsom spa. When local complaints of reveling and 'indecent mirth' on Sundays were ignored, young dissenters – probably encouraged by Fisher and Feake - blew up the cave.

Top: the medieval church by John Beckett. Middle: the intermediate church by John Beckett. Bottom the present church by AE Davidson. Images: Dorking Museum

A church existed in Dorking before Domesday. St Martin's medieval church was probably built in the 12th century. It was largely rebuilt in 1837 to a design by William McIntosh Brookes but that 'intermediate' church lasted only 30 years. The Victorian church of St Martin's was designed by Henry Woodyer (1816-96). Building started in 1866 and the 64 metre spire – a memorial to Bishop Samuel Wilberforce who died whilst out riding at Abinger – was completed in 1877.

John Evelyn, Wotton, and the English Landscape

'The house… may be compared to one of the most tempting and pleasant seates in the Nation" wrote John Evelyn of Wotton House, his family seat just outside Dorking.
Evelyn, who was born in 1620, is best remembered for his diary, which included eye-witness accounts of the Restoration of Charles II in 1660 and the Great Fire of London six years later. His famous diary was allegedly discovered in a laundry basket in Wotton House in 1818.

The Evelyn fortune came from gunpowder milling.
The family acquired the moated manor house in 1579 and acquired the gunpowder mills on the Tillingbourne at Wotton and Abinger. John Evelyn's father, Richard, employed a hundred servants, dressed in green satin doublets with feather-trimmed and braided hats.

John Evelyn travelled Europe studying its gardens.
He designed a formal garden for Henry Howard at neighbouring Albury and his brother created an Italianate garden at Wotton with grottoes, a temple, fountains and an aqueduct from the Tillingbourne. But his lasting influence has been on the landscape surrounding Wotton.

In 'Sylva' (1664) John Evelyn advocated the planting of trees at a time when woodland was being voraciously exploited.
He inherited Wotton on the death of his brother in 1699 but his plans for the estate were largely carried out by his grandson, Sir John Evelyn. Thousands of trees were planted at Wotton and on the neighbouring estates to enhance the landscape. Thus Evelyn played a significant part in the development of what we now think of as the natural landscape of Leith Hill and Friday Street.

Above: Wotton and its Italian garden drawn by John Evelyn. Top: John Evelyn, engraving after Robert Nanteuil, 1650

Dorking's Pilgrim Mother

William Mullins' house on West Street is the only known surviving home of a Pilgrim Father. The building dates from between 1568 and 1610. Mullins bought it with a mortgage in 1612 and sold it in 1619. He ran a successful shoe-making business, so why he risked the voyage to America is not known. He was not one of the 'Saints', the religious separatists who rejected organised worship and who initiated the voyage, but one of the 'Strangers' who were recruited to fund the crossing.

Mullins travelled with his wife Alice, servant Robert Carter, daughter Priscilla, and young son Joseph. (Two grown up children remained in England.) He took a large quantity of business stock; his would have been one of the first businesses in the new colony. The Mayflower landed at Cape Cod in November 1620 and the New Plymouth settlement was established. Disease soon carried off many settlers. Mullins died on February 21st 1621, three months after landing, followed by Alice, Joseph, and Robert Carter. Priscilla, however, survived.

In 1622 Priscilla married John Alden, a cooper from Harwich, Essex, who was responsible for the ship's barrels. Two hundred years later she became a national heroine with the publication of Longfellow's 'The Courtship of Miles Standish'. The poem has Alden proposing marriage on behalf of his superior, Captain Standish, whereupon Priscilla says *'Why don't you speak for yourself, John?'*

Alden and Priscilla and their 10 children settled in the newly established town of Duxbury and John became Deputy Governor of the colony. In the United States Priscilla is revered as a founder of the nation; two US presidents, John Adams and his son, John Quincy Adams, claim descent from the Aldens. Both the Aldens' house in Duxbury, Massachusetts and Mullins' house in Dorking survive as places of pilgrimage for Mayflower descendants.

Above: postcard depicting Priscilla Mullins and John Alden by JPG Ferris, 1907. Image: the John Alden Kindred of America

Left: Mullins' house consists of four gabled 'town houses', timber-framed with two and a half overhanging upper storeys above the ground floor. The brick and tiles are later additions. Drawing by AC Fare, Dorking Museum

Right: Resin model of William Mullins.

Buried in the Country

'Over the whole Wild of Kent and Sussex it is the same, the corn is cheap at the barn because it cannot be carried out, and dear in the market because it cannot be brought in,' wrote Daniel Defoe (*c.* 1660-1731) who appears to have been educated in Dorking for a time. For much of the year travel into Dorking was difficult.

Chart Lane – typical of the rutted and banked up lanes. Image: George Gardiner, Dorking Museum

Stane Street had disappeared into the clay and since Saxon times Dorking's main route south went via Coldharbour to Ockley. But it was *'a shocking, steep ravine, quite impassable for wheels',* with deep furrows cut into the soft greensand. The alternative via Newdigate was churned into a quagmire and the direct track across the Holmwood was worse. Often the only things that could be brought to market were those that could be driven on foot. To the north the situation was not much better. The River Mole had to be crossed at Burford and coaches were often abandoned in favour of horseback for the crossing of the Downs.

For the farmers of the surrounding villages the markets of London, and sometimes even Dorking, were inaccessible. Corn was expensive in Dorking because of the difficulty of getting it there. Timber from Holmwood and Ashcombe Wood lay at the roadside all winter, taking years to reach the Thames. Something would have to be done.

In 1755 Dorking and Horsham landowners petitioned Parliament to be allowed to build a new highway.

This picture of horses hauling timber out of the Weald clay in the early 20th century - the laden wagon sunk into the sodden ground - shows the conditions that local farmers struggled with to get anything to market before the building of the turnpike road.

JAMES RAZEL'S
Dorking Waggon

Sets out from his Yard, DORKING, every MONDAY, WEDNESDAY, and FRIDAY Morning, at Eight o'Clock, to the GEORGE and WHITE HART INNS, BOROUGH, from whence it returns every TUESDAY, THURSDAY, and SATURDAY Morning at Ten o'Clock :—Carries Goods to and from

DORKING, | LETHERHEAD, | EPSOM, | WESTCOT, | WOTTON, | CAPEL,
MICKLEHAM, | ASHTEAD, | EWELL, | ABINGER, | OCKLEY, | NEWDIGATE.

J. RAZEL most respectfully returns his grateful acknowledgments to the Nobility, Gentry and others, for the generous support they have afforded him since he commenced business, and assures them their favors will continue to meet with the same attention as heretofore.

Will not be accountable for Money, Plate, Jewels, Writings, Glass, or any other Parcel above the value of Five Pounds, unless entered as such, and paid for accordingly.

Between the 1820s and the 1840s Razel's horse-drawn wagon carried goods to and from London 3 times a week. Even on the new turnpike road a fully laden wagon pulled by 8 horses took all day to reach London. The man walking behind is probably carrying a stick or blunderbuss to protect the wagon's valuable goods. Trade card, about 1830: Dorking Museum

The Turnpike Road

The Horsham and Epsom Turnpike Act 1755 allowed local landowners to set up a trust to construct a new road.

The Evelyns of Wotton and the Howards of the Deepdene were amongst those who borrowed money secured against future tolls to fund construction.

From Leatherhead the new road followed the River Mole to Mickleham. At the Fox and Hounds (now the Burford Bridge Hotel) it entered the town from the north-east across Denbies. From South Street it climbed Holmwood Common to where St John's church now stands. Descending to what is now mid-Holmwood, it continued towards Beare Green, Capel and Horsham. There were toll gates before Dorking at Giles Green, on Flint Hill and at Holmwood Corner.

Travellers on foot did not pay tolls, except for baggage. One shilling and sixpence was payable for a coach pulled by up to 6 horses, a shilling for a coach pulled by up to four horses and sixpence for one pulled by one or two horses. Wagons and carts paid a shilling, laden animals two pennies, droves of cattle ten pennies per score (12) and calves or sheep five pennies per score.

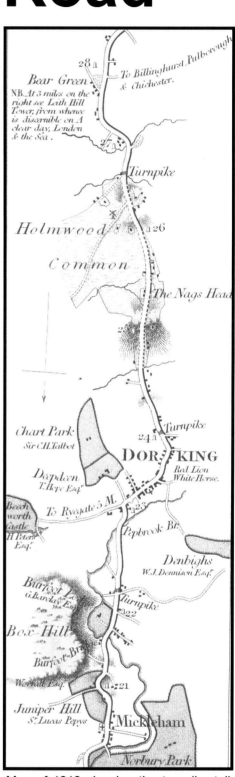

Map of 1818 showing the turnpike toll gates. The rises, particularly onto Holmwood Common, were steep and the descents could be treacherous. Several deaths are recorded under the wheels of runaway wagons.

The toll gate at Giles Green, near the Beehive to the north of the modern Pixham roundabout. Local people tried to avoid the charges, keeping to the by-ways or avoiding the tollgates. The town's other roads were maintained by the parish and parishioners had to work on the roads for a certain number of days a year – unless they were wealthy enough to provide a horse and wagon instead. Image: Dorking Museum

100 GUINEAS
REWARD.

GENERAL POST-OFFICE,
16th July, 1827.

WHEREAS on the Night of Thursday the 12th Instant, about a Quarter-past Ten o'Clock, the Driver with the Mail between Leather-head and Dorking, was feloniously stopped by two Men on the King's Highway, between Leatherhead and Dorking, opposite Givon's Grove, when the Men fired two Pistols at the Driver, and severely wounded him.

The Men are stated to have been dressed in dark Clothes.

WHOEVER will come forward and give such information as may lead to the apprehension and conviction of the Offenders, shall receive a Reward of

One Hundred
GUINEAS.

A Ramrod was found near the spot, and is supposed to have dropped from the Pistol of one of the Offenders.

If either of the Persons concerned in the said Felonious Attack, or any Person knowing thereof will surrender himself, and make discovery whereby the other Offender or Offenders may be apprehended and brought to justice, such Discoverer will be entitled to the said Reward, and will also receive His Majesty's most gracious Pardon.

BY COMMAND,

FRANCIS FREELING,
SECRETARY.

Poster offering a reward for information about a highway robbery between Dorking and Leatherhead, 1827
Trunks on the back of coaches were particularly vulnerable to pilfering when the coach stopped to change horses at inns along the way, and coaches were vulnerable to armed robbery, particularly on the lawless Holmwood stretch. Post office officials were forbidden to put mail bags on the coach until the coachman could show that his pistols were loaded.

What the Dickens?

Dickens was a frequent visitor to Dorking. He set scenes from The Pickwick Papers in the town, modelling the character of Tony Weller on the coach proprietor, William Broad (1789-1862), and the Marquis of Granby inn on the King's Head in North Street.

William Broad, attributed to Dorking artist, John Beckett. All images: Dorking Museum.

Above: The Bull's Head in South Street by John Beckett. A coach can be seen ready to depart. Below: The King's Head in North Street c1898, model for Dickens' Marquis of Granby.

'The Marquis of Granby' in Mrs Weller's time was quite a model of a roadside public house of the best class – just large enough to be convenient and small enough to be snug.'

William Broad's London coach left the Bull's Head in South Street at 7am, reaching the Spread Eagle in Gracechurch Street in 3 hours, returning at 7pm the same evening. The horses were changed at Epsom and Tooting. Merchants and bankers of the town paid fares of 5 shillings (outside) and 7 shillings (inside) one way. Broad, in common with Weller, was genial, witty, smartly-dressed, quick-tempered and poorly-educated. He was known as 'Old Hold Hard!' for his cry to the coachman to 'Hold Hard!' each morning whilst waiting for the strike of seven.

Describing his inspiration, Dickens wrote that: 'The crow drops from Ranmore Hill upon Dorking, which stands close to the old Roman Road... The literary pilgrim looks in vain for his special throne, the Marquis of Granby. The famed house where the fatal widow beguiled old Weller, and where the Shepherd, after imbibing too deeply of his special vanity, was cooled in the horse trough is gone. Let the pilgrim be informed that the real 'Markis', was the King's Head... a great coaching house on the Brighton Road in the old days, and where many a smoking team drew up when Sammywell was young. Long before old Weller mounted his chariot throne, Dorking was a quiet place, much frequented by London merchants... who came down to see Box Hill.'

A Market Town

The new turnpike connected Dorking to London and the south coast, making it easier to travel.

Wood and corn came up from Sussex; pigs and sheep were driven along its route. Dorking hens were sent up to London weekly and the livestock market saw the High Street filled with cattle, sheep and pigs. Access to Dorking's market brought prosperity to farms along the route and landowners raised their rents.

Inns were set up to provide food, lodgings and stabling. Wheelwrights and blacksmiths traded all along the route. By the 1820s the turnpike was carrying four local and sixteen through coaches a day to London - from Horsham, Arundel, Worthing and Bognor.

The market house stood on the High Street next to the Red Lion inn. The town jail was housed in the upper storey.

The Guildford to Reigate road, which remained in a poor state, prevented Dorking from sharing in Guildford's canal-based prosperity. And when newly improved roads between London and Sussex bypassed the town, the importance of its market declined. The market hall fell into a ruinous condition as Dorking's importance as a market centre declined, becoming an eyesore blocking the way through the town. It was demolished in 1813. The Duke of Norfolk, who owned the manor, promised Dorking a new market house but, though the old building materials were sold and the proceeds paid to his agent, the Duke died before work started. Eventually the fund was used to pay for paving of the town.

Dorking market hall by Philip Daws. Image: Dorking Museum

Above and below: the market in the High Street in about 1900. Images: Dorking Museum

The 'Greatest Market for Poultry in England'

So claimed John Aubrey in his *Natural History and Antiquities of the County of Surrey* begun in 1673.

Local farmers' wives bred the large eating 'Dorkings', with their distinctive fifth toe. They were 'crammed' by 'fatters' and brought to the Thursday market in crates, then transported to London by 'higglers'. The eggs were popular too: in 1900 it was reported that something was amiss with Queen Victoria when even the white Dorking eggs served for her breakfast could not make her comfortable.

Top: Dorking cockerel with St Martin's spire and Leith Hill tower by Peter Barnard. Below: The Silver-Grey Dorking on an advert for Dorking Sauce, 1855 Images: Dorking Museum

The breed topped its class in the Zoological Society's first poultry show in London in 1845. Breeders refined the Dorking's colour and physique for competition. The original Grey Dorkings were speckled white, grey and black, with white legs and black tails. White Dorkings were pure white and Edward Lear depicts a lady 'talking to some milk-white hens of Dorking' in his poem *'The Courtship of the Yonghy Bonghy Bo.'* Coloured Dorkings had a salmon breast, brown wing feathers and a black back; the Silver Grey cock had a silvery-white neck, back and wings with a black tail and breast; the hen was silver-grey with a salmon breast. The Cuckoo Dorking was light grey with blue-grey pencilling.

The 'five-claw'd un' has declined in popularity but remains a popular specialist breed. In 1880 the town football club became known as the Chicks. In 1894 the bird appeared on the town seal and in 1951 the chamber of commerce erected cockerel signs on the approaches to the town. Numerous societies have adopted the bird as their emblem.

'The Sweetest Air in England'

In 1649 the Duke of Norfolk's surveyor remarked on Dorking's *'pleasant hills and... salubrious air'*. In 1652 the Duke's son created a small estate at 'Dibden' (Deepdene).

By the 1740s word had spread. Emmanuel Bowen's map proclaimed the air of 'Darking' the sweetest in England. As travel grew swifter and more comfortable, the new wealthy of London built country residences within coaching distance of their business interests. Farms were incorporated into the estates of merchants and financiers who sought to 'improve' the landscape. Chart Park had hanging gardens, Bury Hill ornamental lakes and the Deepdene an ornamental ruin. Elements of these naturalistic but artificial park landscapes can still be seen today.

Mowing the lawn at Bury Hill, c1910. Image: Dorking Museum

Decorators at Bury Hill, c1900. Image: Dorking Museum

Moules Map (right) shows Dorking surrounded by the estates of wealthy London merchants.

Norbury Park

Norbury Park house was built in 1766 for the art critic William Locke. It was later home to Sir Leopold Salomons who gave Box Hill to the nation in 1914, and to the birth control pioneer, Marie Stopes. Image, below, artist unknown

Bury Hill

In 1735 Edward Walter bought up numerous farms to create the Bury Hill estate. From 1812 it was home to the Southwark brewing family, the Barclays. Its ornamental lakes survive as fishing lakes. Image, right, by JP Neale, 1829

Betchworth Castle

The fortified manor house of the manor of West Betchworth was traditionally home to the lords of that manor. It was bought in 1798 by banker, Henry Peters. It stretched from the zigzag at Box Hill to beyond Blackbrook and Sir John Soane designed additions to the house. Swallowed into the Deepdene estate, the castle now lies in ruins. Image, left, by GF Prosser

Denbies

Jonathan Tyers, owner of the pleasure gardens in Vauxhall, bought Denbies farmhouse in 1734 and converted it into a landed estate. It was later rebuilt by Thomas Cubitt, the master builder and is now home to England's largest vineyard. Image, left, c1829 by JP Neale

Deepdene

Established by the Howard family and home to two Dukes of Norfolk, the Deepdene was the grandest of Dorking's estates and eventually Chart Park and Betchworth Castle became part of its lands. Photograph, right, c1890

Juniper Hall

The 18th century house that was once home to wealthy French émigrés escaping the French Revolution is now a field studies centre. Image, left, by 'Dibden', c1844

Burford Lodge
Burford Lodge, at the foot of Box Hill, was built in the 1770s and was later the home of the horticulturalist, Sir Trevor Lawrence. Drawing, below, by TA Prior c1845

Chart Park

Henry Talbot founded Chart Park on the old Deepdene vineyard in 1746 with money made with the East India Company in China. The house was pulled down in 1814 and its park was incorporated into the neighbouring Deepdene estate. Undated drawing, below, reproduced by permission of Surrey History Centre

Milton Court

Milton Court started life as a dower house. It was rebuilt in 1611 by the Evelyn family. The house contains a splendid Jacobean staircase. Photograph, above right, c1905

By the end of the 19th century there were scores of smaller mansions surrounding Dorking, including Anstie Grange, home of Admiral Sir Leopold Heath, Broome Hall, home of Frederick Pennington MP (both near Coldharbour), Abinger Hall, home of Lord Farrer and Lyne House, near Capel, home of the Broadwood family of piano manufacturers. Images: Dorking Museum

The Howards of the Deepdene

In 1652 Charles Howard, son of the Earl of Arundel, inherited a share in the manor of Dorking.

He settled at 'Dibden' on the eastern edge of the town. Initially he lived in a relatively humble manner. But after the Restoration of the British monarchy in 1660 he built himself a large house. There he studied natural history, conducted experiments in his laboratory, and created an Italianate garden with rare plants and grottoes that was admired by the antiquary and biographer John Aubrey and the writer, John Evelyn.

In the 1760s Charles Howard's grandson, also called Charles, built a mansion on the 100 acre estate.
The younger Charles became 10th Duke of Norfolk in 1777. He spent his summers at the Deepdene and his winters in London.

The 11th Duke abandoned the Deepdene in 1790.
He intended to build a new mansion at Newdigate but renovated Arundel Castle instead. On his death his body was brought from Norfolk House in London to Burford Bridge, just outside Dorking, where it was joined by a cavalcade of heralds, nobility and attendants, who followed his body to St Martin's church.

The Dukes of Norfolk sold the manor of Brockham to the Hope family in the early 19th century but remained absentee landlords of the manor of Dorking until the 1950s when they sold all their Dorking properties. The Norfolk and Arundel connection is recalled in many local street names.

Charles Howard, 11th Duke of Norfolk was known as the 'Protestant Duke'. A slovenly man, he disliked washing so much that he had to be washed by his servants whilst in a drunken stupor. Image: James Lonsdale

The dramatist Richard Brinsley Sheridan (1751-1816) was allowed the use of the Deepdene by the 11th Duke. He went on to purchase the estate at Polesden Lacey near Dorking which is now owned by the National Trust. Image: Karl Anton Hickel

Thomas Hope and the Deepdene

Thomas Hope (1769-1831)

In 1808 Thomas Hope bought the Deepdene. Hope used the Deepdene to showcase his art collections, and interests in connoisseurship and Neo-Classicalism.

Five years later his brother, Henry Philip Hope, bought the neighbouring Chart Park and gave it to Thomas who added it to the Deepdene estate. Hope demolished the mansion at Chart Park and re-modelled the Deepdene along classical lines. He added a sculpture gallery and a kitchen/dairy topped with an Italianate loggia (a type of open sided extension often added to large houses). In 1833 the Deepdene was described as the finest Italianate villa in England by J.C Loudon in the *Gardener's Magazine.*

Thomas Hope's contribution to the development of art and architecture in Britain has been widely recognized. The Deepdene became famous as the resort of men of letters and people of fashion.

Thomas Hope's son, Henry Thomas Hope (1808-1862), undertook further remodeling to the house, creating a sumptuous high renaissance palazzo.

He incorporated the Betchworth Castle estate into the Deepdene in 1834, resulting in a land-holding 12 miles in circumference that stretched from Box Hill to Brockham with a private toll road. The castle was partially dismantled by Hope to create a picturesque ruin.

Thomas Hope was born in Amsterdam where his Scottish-Dutch banking family was based. The Hopes moved to London when French revolutionary forces occupied the Netherlands. He travelled widely in the study of art. Hope is interred at the Deepdene in the grade II* listed Mausoleum that he built following the death of his 7 year-old son in 1817. The mausoleum, which has fish-scale fanlights and a stone vaulted roof, was closed in 1941 and later buried up to its pediment. In 1960 Hope's descendent, the Duke of Newcastle, gave the surrounding ground to Dorking as public open space.

The terrace, with its temple (erected by Hope in 1814 at the highest point of the Deepdene to commemorate his brother's gift of Chart Park), was purchased in 1943 by the Dorking & Leith Hill Preservation Society and given to the people of Dorking.
Painting by Henry Bone

Left: Benjamin Disraeli (1804-1881) was a frequent visitor to his friend Henry Hope at the Deepdene. He often stayed there with fellow followers of his 'Young England' movement and with Hope's encouragement he turned his political thoughts into the novel *Coningsby* (1844), writing much of it at the Deepdene. He acknowledges in his introduction that it was conceived there and he dedicated it to Hope. This bust was made on the site of the Museum at the Dorking Foundry.
Right: the Deepdene by William Bartlett

Decline of the Deepdene

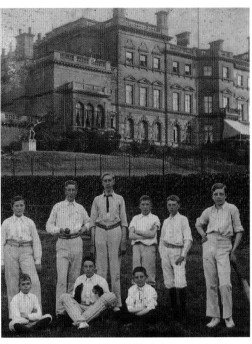

Henry Hope's grandson Francis, the 8th Duke of Newcastle (1866-1941), only used Deepdene for shooting parties.

In 1892 Francis and his guests shot 2,812 pheasants, partridges and rabbits there. He let the house to the dowager Duchess of Marlborough. The Duchess's nephew Winston Churchill regularly took the train down to Dorking to visit his aunt as a young man. The Prince of Wales was another of the Duchess's regular guests.

Above: The boys of St Martin's choir playing cricket at Deepdene, c1905.
Below right: Lilian (Lily) Spencer-Churchill, Duchess of Marlborough.
Below left: The Deepdene Hotel postcard, 1920s. Images: Dorking Museum

The seeds of Deepdene's decline were sown in 1849 with the Redhill to Reading railway line cutting through the north of the estate. This was followed in 1867 with the London to Horsham line to the east of the estate. The house was occupied by the military in the First World War. By the 1920s developments in road and rail travel had significantly impacted on the Deepdene. The Duke finally sold the estate in the 1920s. The land nearest to the stations was used for housing and the house became a 90-bedroomed hotel. But the construction of the Dorking bypass in the 1930s brought a busy road within sight of its façade. In 1939 the house was bought by the Southern Railway to be its wartime headquarters during the Second World War.

With most of the estate's land sold, consumed by housing, roads or railway tracks, Thomas Hope's great mansion fell into disrepair. The house was demolished in 1969 and an office block erected on the site.

The demolition of Deepdene and the office building that replaced it, by Dorothy Parsons. Images: Dorking Museum

34

Thomas Cubitt and Denbies

Denbies, a large estate overlooking Dorking, was established in the 18th century by Jonathan Tyers, owner of the Vauxhall Pleasure Gardens in London.

Tyers laid out the grounds at Denbies with a temple and a clock which struck minutes rather than hours, skulls marking out pathways and solemn figures reminding the living of the inevitability of death.

In 1827 a builder named Thomas Cubitt, the son of a Norfolk carpenter, supervised the building of Polesden Lacey, just north of Denbies. Two decades later, having amassed a fortune from the building of Bloomsbury, Belgravia and parts of Buckingham Palace in London and Osborne House on the Isle of Wight, Cubitt bought the 3,900 acre Denbies estate. Cubitt rebuilt the original house with a brick and stucco mansion of almost 100 rooms. Prince Albert visited to plant a symbolic tree.

Denbies mansion in about 1860. Cubitt had his own railway siding at Dorking for the delivery of construction materials. He used the Ranmore chalk pits on the estate for the lime mortar.

Cubitt planted trees and holly to cover the bare chalk of his estate and much of the landscape to the north east of Dorking can be said to be Cubitt's work. But Cubitt had little time to enjoy his retreat: in 1855 he died, leaving a fortune of over £1 million. Queen Victoria said of Cubitt that 'a better, kinder-hearted man never breathed'.

A statue of Cubitt, who always insisted on being called a builder and not an architect, stands opposite Dorking Halls.
Another stands in London's Denbigh Street.

Workmen at Ranmore on the Denbies estate in about 1900. The estate employed several hundred in its farms, grounds and quarries and had its own school, fire-brigade and church, St Barnabas at Ranmore.

Fanny Burney and the French Émigrés

Fanny Burney by Edward Francis Burney

In September 1792 a party of wealthy French émigrés arrived in Mickleham near Dorking.

Escaping the French Revolution, they crossed the channel in small boats. Their stay at Juniper Hall, near Dorking, and a nearby cottage was made possible by William Lock of Norbury Park, a wealthy art collector.

The British writer, Fanny Burney, was a frequent visitor to Lock's mansion as her sister lived in Mickleham. Burney sympathized with the refugees' plight, developing a close relationship with one of the émigrés, General Alexandre D'Arblay who taught her French and introduced her to the writer and salon hostess Madame de Stael. Stael's relationship with Comte Louis de Narbonne, a former French minister for war, attracted local gossip. Fanny's father disapproved of the émigrés and forbade Fanny from visiting them because of Madame de Stael's reputation.

Mme de Stael by Francois Gerard

Fanny married General D'Arblay at Mickleham church in 1793. After their wedding they rented the Hermitage at Bookham, where the General attempted gardening to feed the family.

The success of Fanny's novel, *Camilla* enabled the couple to build Camilla Cottage on one of Lock's fields. The cottage was completed in 1797. In 1802 Fanny and her young son joined the General who had returned to France. The family was never able to return to Camilla Cottage. When they arrived back in England in 1812 Lock was dead and with no formal lease for the land they lost the property. Fanny spent the rest of her life in London and Bath.

Juniper Hall c1844

Prince Charles Maurice de Tallyrand was another of the émigrés at Mickleham. He was a hugely influential diplomat in post-revolutionary Europe. Portrait by Pierre-Paul Prud'hon

The Broadwoods of Lyne

Horses and hounds outside Lyne House. Image: Dorking Museum

The piano manufacturer James Schudi Broadwood bought Lyne Farm, Capel, in 1799.

The family firm was England's foremost piano manufacturer. Beethoven, Haydn, Chopin and Liszt all used Broadwood pianos. Broadwood turned Lyne into a grand family home, buying up surrounding land in Capel, Newdigate and Rusper. In 1864 his son, Henry Fowler Broadwood, arrived in Lyne with his 9 children.

Henry's eldest daughter Bertha Broadwood founded the Cottage Benefit Nursing Association in 1883.

The Association trained working-class nurses in the Holt-Ockley method (named after the nearby village). The method sent nurses into the homes of Capel and Holmwood women to live with them, attending to domestic duties as well as medical care. This enabled the patients to rest. The local organisation soon went national with branches all over the country and a London training scheme. Bertha was a vigorous campaigner in Dorking against the vote for women.

Bertha Broadwood in 1903. By permission of the Broadwood Trust

Bertha's youngest sister Lucy Broadwood was a pioneering collector and publisher of folk songs.

She collaborated on several influential publications and was a founder, with Cecil Sharpe and Ralph Vaughan Williams, of the English Folk Song Society whose journal she edited. Many of the songs that she preserved were collected in the Surrey villages around Lyne. An accomplished singer, composer and accompanist she was also one of the founders of the Leith Hill Musical Festival. In recognition of her contribution to the preservation of English folk traditions Morris men dance in Rusper church, where she is buried, every May 1st.

Left: Lucy Broadwood. By permission of Surrey History Centre

Poverty and the Workhouse

Stoneheal Cottage in South Holmwood was one of two cottages with gardens, orchards and rights of common kept by Dorking Overseer of the Poor Nathanial Wix in the 1790s. There he provided work to paupers in return for their keep.

The wealth of the mansions was in great contrast to the impoverished countryside. Agricultural labourers were paid only when work was available. They were seldom far from poverty.

The early 19th century was hard. The innovations of the agricultural revolution were ineffective on clay soils. Local farmers could not compete with market prices once cheap corn could be brought in from elsewhere. Fields were withdrawn from production and labourers put out of work. By the 1820s many families were relying on the poor rates for survival.

Though there was a workhouse in South Street the parish often made maintenance payments to poor families. But the mass poverty of the 1820s was a huge burden on rate payers. Dorking parish officers tried to persuade farmers to take on labourers at subsistence rates, but this forced wages lower as struggling farmers let go higher paid labourers. And as poor rates increased cashless smallholders were forced into bankruptcy, creating further dependence on the rates.

In 1834 the Dorking Poor Law Union was established, covering Abinger, Capel, Dorking, Westcott, Coldharbour, Effingham, Mickleham, Newdigate, Ockley and Wotton. In 1841 the new Union Workhouse was built on the Dorking Hospital site. 'Outside' relief would only be given in exceptional circumstances; those in poverty would now have to enter the workhouse.

The almshouses on Cotmandene provided relief to a small number of elderly people. Painting by J. Hassell

THE
Manor of Dorking,
𝔍𝔫 𝔱𝔥𝔢 𝔠𝔬𝔲𝔫𝔱𝔶 𝔬𝔣 𝔖𝔲𝔯𝔯𝔢𝔶.

At a Meeting of the COPYHOLDERS of the said MANOR held at the RED LION INN, in DORKING, on FRIDAY the 12th of APRIL, 1822;

A Proposal was made on the part of His GRACE the DUKE of NORFOLK, Lord of the said Manor, that the Copyholders should be allowed to cut Furzes and Fern on the HOLMWOOD, within the said Manor, the same being set out by a Person to be appointed by the Lord of the said Manor for that purpose, for which *One Shilling* be paid for each hundred of Furzes and each Waggon load of Fern, which was approved of and agreed to.

And, it was the opinion of this Meeting, that there should be no Brick Kiln on the waste of this Manor in the Holmwood, and that no Clay be dug on the Holmwood to supply any Brick Kiln on private Property; but that the Pottery now used by GEORGE MILLER, be allowed to be continued so long as he continues to occupy it, or till notice shall be given him to desist, he using it in a proper manner.

And that no Earth whatever be taken from the Holmwood by any Person on any pretence whatever.

William Bray,
𝔖𝔱𝔢𝔴𝔞𝔯𝔡 𝔬𝔣 𝔱𝔥𝔢 𝔠𝔬𝔲𝔯𝔱𝔰 𝔬𝔣 𝔱𝔥𝔢 𝔰𝔞𝔦𝔡 𝔐𝔞𝔫𝔬𝔯.

LANGLEY, PRINTER, DORKING.

Holmwood Common came under pressure in this period from desperate people pillaging its resources – illegally burning lime, stealing gravel, ferns and bracken – and from smugglers and highway robbers. It was, claimed millionaire Thomas Hope, *'a harbour for thieves, vagabonds and idle and disorderly people'*. He supported enclosing it, claiming that selling it off would remove the opportunity for idling and create more legitimate work, so relieving costs to ratepayers. But the argument prevailed that this would throw households with legitimate rights of common into destitution, unable to survive without rights to take wood and graze their animals, resulting in even higher poor rates.

'Bread or Blood!'

By 1830 desperate men were living on hills and commons, surviving through crime.

Anger at lack of work and low wages was directed at the town authorities – largely insulated against the poverty of the countryside by virtue of their London interests.

In November 1830 labourers ran through Dorking shouting 'bread or blood!' Haystacks were burned at Trouts Farm and a mob gathered at the Wotton Hatch. On 22nd November Dorking magistrates asked for the cavalry to be quartered in town. Staves were taken into the Red Lion and pikes burned to prevent their use. Townsmen swore in 114 special constables. Hundreds stormed the town. As magistrate James Broadwood appealed to the crowd outside the Red Lion a riderless horse appeared, packed with broomsticks. Rioters seized the sticks and attacked the hotel before being chased out of town by the cavalry.

Emigration and immigration

In the spring of 1832 the Dorking Emigration scheme arranged for 72 people to join a ship bound for Canada. The parish had concluded that the land would never support all those available to work. Two years later the poor relief was reduced and magistrate Charles Barclay was burned in effigy.

It was immigration rather than emigration that eventually alleviated Dorking's poverty. As the beauties of the area grew renowned the well-to-do moved in, bringing employment in their mansions, villas and gardens. They brought incomes from other activities, their estate farms subsidised by trading, brewing or banking. By the late 1830s Dorking was acclaimed a London in miniature 'possessing shops little inferior in taste… to those of Cheapside and the Strand'.

The writings of Thomas Malthus (1766-1834) may have influenced the parish authorities in their decision to encourage emigration. Malthus was born at the Rookery in Westcott (below). In his Essays on Population (1798-1826) he proposed that poverty was inevitable as population would always increase more rapidly than the means of subsistence. He concluded that poverty and misery were necessary to keep population growth in check. Drawing of the Rookery by H Gastineau.

Notice.

It has been made to appear to the Magistrates acting for the Hundred of Wotton, that Hand-bills have been circulated and stuck up in three of the Parishes of this Hundred, tending to excite discontent in the minds of the labouring Classes, and to create dissatisfaction and ill-will towards the Government, through the means of deception and misrepresentation, the Magistrates,—with a view to protect the honest labourer from the mischievous designs of men, known in this case to be strangers to the County, and to have no common interest with those whom they would mislead,—feel themselves called upon, in their characters of conservators of the public peace, and as the true friends of the labourers amongst whom they live, to warn them against the objects of these strangers, who, if they should excite them into violations of the law, would, as has been done on so many recent occasions, leave them to suffer the consequences of crime, which, but for such influence, they might never have thought of committing.

This caution,—given in the spirit of kindness and good-will, and in the most anxious desire to prevent the spread of those evils, which have so lately afflicted the adjacent Counties,—is called forth in consequence of its having come to the knowledge of the Magistrates, that an Agent, employed for that purpose by an Inhabitant Shopkeeper of HORSHAM, was sent on *Wednesday the 22nd. instant*, to distribute and post up Hand-bills of the character herein described, at the Public Houses and other places in the Parishes of CAPEL, OCKLEY and DORKING; and as the Magistrates have reason to believe, that the circulation of these mischievous publications is systematically pursued, they cannot too earnestly beseech the Inhabitants of this Hundred, carefully to guard themselves against these and any other attempts of designing Men, to render them the dupes of misrepresentations, which can have no honest purpose or intention.

BY ORDER OF THE MAGISTRATES,

THOMAS HART,
CLERK.

Dorking, Dec. 28th, 1830.

LANGLEY, PRINTER, DORKING.

Working Town

Though the economy was still largely agricultural, in the 19th century much of what was traded in Dorking was produced in the town's forges, foundry and workshops.

Saubergue's ironmonger's was on the High Street. It produced pots, pans, kettles, hods and washing coppers. The business employed 30 blacksmiths, gunsmiths, whitesmiths, coppersmiths and braziers.

John Fuller began work there at the age of 9 in 1842, stoking the fire and greasing tools. His day began at 6 by the light of a whale-oil lamp and continued, with breaks for breakfast, lunch and tea, until 7pm, 6 days a week.

Saubergue's was taken over by Stone & Turner, whose foundry was on the site of Dorking Museum.

Attlee's feed store opposite Pump Corner.

All images: Dorking Museum

Foreman of the forge at Ansell Road, George Green, lost his life on the Titanic. He was heading to a new life in America. The town boasted numerous blacksmiths, wheelwrights and several coach-builders.

Above: Sign for Attlee's feed store. Attlee's corn and seed merchants' was established in Dorking in 1788, and the family operated Parsonage Mill on the Pippbrook. The business remained in the family for nearly 200 years, becoming J&W Attlee in the 1880s. Below: Dorking Co-operative store, South Street c1905

Chalk and Lime

Used as an ingredient in making mortar, Dorking lime was considered by many to be the best in the county, and possibly the best in the country.

Mixed with sand and water, Dorking lime was used to fix together the stones and bricks which make up Somerset House and the Bank of England in London. Its hardening qualities in water were so good that it was also used in the construction of West India and London Docks in the port of London.

Lime is converted from chalk by burning in kilns. For generations farmers had burned chalk from the North Downs in small kilns in the corners of their fields, spreading the resulting lime across their land to improve its quality. The Dorking chalk pits at Bradley Farm, in the neighbouring manor of Bradley, were in operation by the 1600s. The chalk was burned at six large kilns at Chalkpit Lane, off Ranmore Road. Today the household waste site dump occupies part of the site.

With the coming of the turnpike road, Dorking lime could more easily be transported to London. The lime would first be sent by wagon to Kingston, where it was loaded aboard barges and sent along the Thames. On the return journey, coal would be brought to power Dorking's kilns and for household use.

By the early 19th century chalk pits were operating at Brockham and at Betchworth, where the Betchworth Dorking Greystone Lime Company traded on the renowned Dorking name. Production continued until the Second World War but ceased when lighting restrictions came into force.

Dorking limekilns, artist unknown

Above and below: Dorking Greystone Limeworks c1905

Lime workers' cottages, Betchworth around 1910
All images: Dorking Museum

Clay and Bricks

Local clay has been dug for hundreds of years.

In the 1790s George Miller of Ram Alley (Dene Street) obtained permission to dig clay from the common at North Holmwood to produce drain pipes, roof tiles, plant pots, bricks, and chimney pots. The area became known as the Potteries and the village pond is a result of his clay diggings.

Later the clay was used to make bricks.

Kilns were set up at Stubs Farm between Dorking and Holmwood in the 1870s. By the 1920s the Dorking Brick Company's site stretched from North Holmwood to Blackbrook and was surrounded by terraced brick housing. The company employed 60 to 70 men, and used a small steam railway to move bricks about the works.

Dorking bricks were used all over the south-east, in local housing and in the construction of the Middlesex, St Bartholomew's and Surrey County hospitals.

Top right: Harry Leggett's motor lorry at the brickworks
Middle: Brick production at North Holmwood
Bottom: The Dorking Brick Company's offices on the corner of Spook Hill and Holmesdale Road were refaced and extended in 1931 as a showcase for what could be achieved in brick.
Below: Some of the workforce in the 1930s
All images: Dorking Museum

Dorking's Caves

Dorking's caves were all made by humans.

Soft enough to dig by pick and shovel, the 'Folkestone' sands that lie beneath the town do not collapse after digging so they are ideal for the digging of cellars. Similar caverns are found all along the Holmesdale Valley from Redhill to Guildford. The caves were excavated by brewers, grocers, vintners and householders to keep beer, dairy products, wine, and meat cool. They were used until the 1960s

Wine stores in the Wheatsheaf caves. Image: Dorking Museum

Under the old Wheatsheaf pub on the High Street there is a cave which was used for cock-fighting. Beneath Sainsburys' car park there was a huge cave with an elaborately painted interior.

The spectacular South Street Caves, with their galleries and staircases, were probably dug in the late 17th century. Some suggest they were used for secret political meetings or as a refuge for Dorking's religious dissenters but it is more likely that they were excavated as a folly. Follies and grottoes were in vogue during this period; both Charles Howard at the Deepdene and John Evelyn at Albury excavated similar features.

Diagram showing the layout of the South Street caves. Diagram: Richard Selley

Well Shaft

19th c. Wine Vault

Blocked Entrance

Stair Case

19th c. Wine Vault

Entrance & Exit

Lower Mystery Chamber

Scale in Metres

The Dorking Foundry

Stone and Turner's iron & brass foundry occupied the site of Dorking Museum.

The foundry began life as a blacksmith's forge operated by the Bartlett family in the 1820s. By the 1850s the brass and iron foundry was employing 17 men, turning out tools, agricultural equipment, street furniture and decorative goods.

Walter Stone and Henry Turner took on the foundry in the 1880s. They kept retail premises in the High Street. WL Bodman took over the business in 1918.

During the Second World War the foundry was operating 24 hours a day, employing 60 people, 13 of them women. In these years the foundry produced over 4,000 machine tools, 1,800 tons of iron castings and 300,000 screw bomb nose adaptors.

The smaller building close to West Street served as the offices and clocking-in point. The foundry itself operated from the building which now houses the Dorking Museum & Heritage Centre gallery and archive. Remains of the foundry lifting equipment can be seen overhead, running between the office building and its neighbour.

Top: Foundry staff at work, about 1918
Middle: The foundry site in the 1970s
Bottom: manufactured goods from Stone and Turner's foundry for sale in Dorking High Street in the 1890s
All images: Dorking Museum

Bought of STONE & TURNER,
Engineers, Iron and Brass Founders, Smiths.
GENERAL & FURNISHING
Ironmongers.
AGENTS TO ALL IMPLEMENT MAKERS.

Johnstons' Sweepers

A company named the Road Plant Construction Company operated from the site of Dorking Museum in the early 20th century.

It made agricultural equipment and road surface machinery and later moved to Vincent Lane.

In 1924 the company was taken over by Johnston Brothers.

Johnstons had been set up in 1904 at Cannon Street in London to import stone from Germany for road use. With the growth of motor transport Johnstons had moved from the supply of materials into the road maintenance business, making tar spreading machines.

As road use increased Johnstons developed a wide range of road surface machines.

From the Dorking site the company produced innovative gritters, snow ploughs and tar boilers. In 1937 Johnstons produced its first mechanical road surface cleaner, the Johnston Mobile Sweeper and Collector. It was a great advance in sweeper design. During the Second World War Johnstons' snow ploughs were in use at 600 airfields around the country.

Still in business today, Johnstons' factory in Curtis Road produces road sweepers for markets all over the world, employing more than 300 people.

Above: the Johnston Mk1 prototype sweeper on the A24 opposite the Burford Bridge. Photograph by permission of Johnston's Sweepers Right: an early piece of road equipment on the move through Dorking High Street.

Art and Inspiration

Many artists have lived and worked in the villages and hills around Dorking.

Denham Jordan. Image: Dorking Museum

Denham Jordan came to the town in 1849.

A house painter who had worked on the restoration of Clandon Park, he became a naturalist and illustrator. He was best known for the wildlife observations which appeared in Blackwood's Magazine. Signing himself Son of the Marshes, he published ten nature books, including *On Surrey Hills* and *Woodland, Moor and Stream*.

Alfred Charles Jerome Collins arrived in Dorking aged 24.

From East Street, Arundel Road and Horsham Road he exhibited regularly at the Royal Academy, mainly in water-colour and oil. Many of his paintings are of the Dorking and Mole Valley area.

Charles Collins. Image: Dorking Museum

The sculptor Sir Joseph Edgar Boehm divided his time between London and his North Holmwood studio.

His studio sat opposite his mansion, Bentsbrook. Much commissioned by the royal family – he modelled John Brown (who called him Mr Bum) and the royal dogs for Queen Victoria - London is dotted with his work.

In 1885 Christopher Whall moved to Ada Cottage, Blackbrook.

He set up a studio in an outbuilding at the small-holding that he ran with his portrait-painter wife, Florence, in order to master the art of glass making. He became the leading stained-glass artist of the Arts and Crafts movement, collaborating on projects with William Morris.

Sir Joseph Boehm

Lucien Pissarro spent nine months in Coldharbour in 1915/6.

Son of the Impressionist Camillle Pissarro, and founder of the Camden Town group of artists, his views of the village are now held at the Courtauld and the Tate.

John Beckett

John Beckett was the youngest of nine children of John Beckett, tailor and staymaker, of Dorking.

He began his life working for his brother-in-law, a plumber and glazier. In 1833 his father died leaving him three houses adjacent to the Ram public house, on the High Street near Dene Street.

His paintings of Dorking streets form a valuable record of the buildings and inhabitants in the 1830s, particularly in 1835, when the decision was taken to rebuild Dorking's medieval church. Beckett, who was a member of the Vestry, painted fascinating views of its exterior and interior.

There is no evidence that he had any formal artistic training. According to JS Bright's *'History of Dorking'*, 'he followed the business of house-painter and decorator'. Probably this work took him into the houses of the local gentry, where the paintings and 'objets d'art' may have awoken his artistic instincts.

In 1846 and 1847 his landscape paintings were exhibited in London at the British Institution and in 1862 at the Royal Society of British Artists.

Beckett never married and lived at 5, South Street at the foot of Butter Hill. When he died in 1864 he was able to make generous bequests to his sister and nephews and nieces.

Top: John Beckett, courtesy of Mary Day
Middle: West Street and Pump Corner
Below: South Street Images: Dorking Museum

'The Nicest Place'

'...within a prudent distance of town, in England.'

So wrote the playwright Richard Brinsley Sheridan of Dorking in 1797.

As coach travel became faster and more comfortable the town developed a reputation amongst wealthy Londoners as a holiday resort. Its good air and picturesque countryside were recommended to invalids.

The King's Head and the Red Lion inns were famous for their 'Water Souchy', a fish stew made from perch, carp or tench, onions and parsley. The name probably comes from the Dutch *'waterzootje'* as the dish was popular with visiting Dutch merchants.

When the Romantic Movement popularised communing with nature Box Hill became a popular destination: John Keats completed *Endymion* (1818) whilst staying at the Burford Bridge Hotel (then known as the Fox and Hounds); Nelson visited in 1801 and John Stuart Mill rented a cottage at Mickleham in the 1820s.

Locals rented out their houses for the summer, inns hired out horses and carriages, and the town produced its own refreshments, ginger beer and mineral waters.

Box Hill still attracts 850,000 visitors a year.

Box Hill is the setting for one of English literature's best known scenes, the picnic in Jane Austen's *Emma* (1816). Austen knew Box Hill well; she visited her cousin who lived at nearby Great Bookham several times.
Emma's picnic is typical of visits to Box Hill in the early 19th century. The wealthy visitors arrive by carriage and eat in the open air, a recent innovation for the wealthy that gives the event an air of daring.
Image: artist unknown. By permission of the University of Texas

A rambling club on Ranmore. Image: Dorking Museum

The Walking Dunghill

At the top of Box Hill a plaque marks the grave of local eccentric Major Peter Labelliere (1726-1800).

Labelliere by Joseph Wright. Image: Dorking Museum

A deeply pious man who did not drink, eat meat, or allow any paper containing the word 'God' or 'Christ' to be destroyed, Labelliere was a radical thinker who wrote tracts on liberty and social reform. Having spent time in the army he came to Dorking from Chiswick and rented a room at the Hole in the Wall cottage in South Street. Children would follow him through town, so generous was he with pennies to those who could recite the Lord's Prayer or a passage from the scriptures. He would buy clothes for those in need but he was notoriously negligent with his own personal hygiene and was known as the Walking Dunghill.

Box Hill was his favourite place of meditation. He fell in the undergrowth there and lost the sight of one eye at the spot where he was eventually buried. His last wish was that his landlady's children dance on his coffin to show that death was a cause for rejoicing rather than sorrow. The son complied; the daughter would only sit on it.

Major Labelliere was buried, according to his wishes, without religious rites, upside down on Box Hill. A huge crowd attended. It is thought that he chose this position in recognition of St Peter who was crucified upside down. Honouring his belief in the joyfulness of death, for many years people came on the anniversary to visit his grave, to picnic, and to dance.

The Coming of the Railways

In 1849 a railway line between Reading, Guildford and Reigate was built to enable passengers and goods from the Channel ports to connect with existing lines to the Midlands and the West. It ran past Dorking.

A small station (now Dorking West) was built near the town's chalk pits. Two years later Box Hill station (now Dorking Deepdene) opened on the London turnpike road to allow coach travellers to connect in to rail services from coaches travelling the main turnpike road. Though it did not offer a direct route to London the line had a terrible impact on Dorking's road transport businesses as goods could now be carried up to London by rail rather than by horse and wagon. Building materials and coal came in, and bricks and lime went out, by rail.

In 1867 Dorking got a direct route to London, and a third station. The Leatherhead to Horsham line passed east towards Betchworth via a tunnel rather than directly south to avoid the gradients towards Leith Hill.

The railways brought a great influx on new residents into the town. Businesses in London were now within easy reach. The surrounding hills were colonized by those who could afford rail fares and horse taxi rides from the stations at Gomshall, Betchworth and Holmwood. On their slopes woodlands were shaped and exotic trees planted around the grand residences of 'gentlemen'. In town speculative builders put up villas for professionals, civil servants and military men and businesses grew to supply them with goods and services.

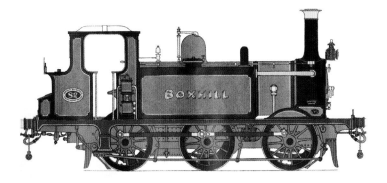

The South Eastern Railway Hotel next to Dorking's first station - now the Pilgrim inn. Below: A train passing Box Hill. Images: Dorking Museum and Mary Day

The London to Brighton and South Coast Railway, which operated the Leatherhead to Horsham line, named locomotives after villages and beauty spots on its routes: Deepdene, Denbies, Dorking, Holmwood and Box Hill. Image: Dorking Museum

Two-horse omnibuses met passengers at the station, though the wealthy had their own carriages and later cars. Dorking's first cabs were run by Eleanor Holden of the Red Lion. Image: Dorking Museum

ON THE OPENING OF THE RAILROAD TO DORKING.

July 1849.

Sure old Time's running on with a step passing fast
For the Railroad to Dorking is opened at last
And where nought save green pastures and Cornfields were found
Now the Train casts its Smoke, Fire and Cinders around

Yes the Railroad is come! In our quiet old Town
People run to and fro, looking out for " the Down"
And the Rustics all gaping with wonder, are still
As the " Four-Twenty-five" rises over the Hill !

Oh, how changed from the Time when with Trappings so fair
BROAD'S grey Team rattled by through the clear Summer air
And himself on the Coach-box so trim and so neat
Cracked his Whip as they cheerily dashed up the Street

Surely Changings and Shiftings on all sides we view
For the Times are all changed and we change with them too
Where our Sires were content to arrive there in FOUR
We complain if we don't get to Town in an Hour.

And now that our Railroad has opened so true
May it do all the good we hoped it would do
May it further our pleasure our Trade our renown
Be of use to our Gentry, our Tradesmen, OUR TOWN.

W. H. HART.

Poem celebrating the opening of the railway to Dorking. The 3rd verse refers to coachman
William Broad who ran his coaches to London from the Bull's Head. Image: Dorking Museum

Day Trippers

Direct rail travel reduced the journey time from London to an hour in 1867, bringing unprecedented numbers of day visitors to the hills around Dorking.

On a fine bank holiday in the 1890s up to 5,000 day-trippers would arrive in Dorking by rail - and 2,000 or more by carriage, horse-bus or cycle. Rail companies advertised the beauty of the Surrey Hills on posters. Leisure guides described walks from the railway stations with rail fares advertised in the back. Stations were named after beauty spots: 'Westhumble and Box Hill' and 'Holmwood for Leith Hill'.

Box Hill and Leith Hill became London's playground and they remain so to this day. Cyclists came touring; youth groups, like the early Scouts and the Kibbo Kift, hiked and camped; in Newdigate the early labour movement held socialist holiday camps at Cudworth. And benevolent philanthropists like the Pethick-Lawrences of Holmwood and Sir Arthur Brooke (of the Brooke Bond tea fortune) of Leylands in Abinger, set up hostels and holiday homes to enable poorer Londoners to benefit from the clean air. Holmbury St Mary housed one of the first youth hostels.

By the 1930s rail passengers had been joined by motor coaches and motor buses. On Whit Monday 1947 14,000 passengers alighted at Box Hill station and 12,000 more at Dorking North, with more arriving by bicycle, bus and car.

Above: Box Hill, around 1916. Middle: Burford Bridge, 1920s. Bottom: London bus poster
Images: London Transport Museum

DORKING
THROUGHOUT FARE 1/6
From CLAPHAM COMMON

ROUTE 70
DAILY
PASSING MERTON, EWELL, EPSOM, ASHTEAD, LEATHERHEAD, MICKLEHAM, BOXHILL.

'After we had conquered the hill itself, I saw a sight that would transport a stoic; a sight that looked like enchantment and a vision beatific! Beneath us, lay open to our view, all the wilds of Surrey and Sussex, and a great part of Kent, admirably diversified in every part of them with woods, and fields of corn and pasture, and everywhere adorned with stately rows of trees.'
John Dennis, dramatist and critic, around 1700

Tourists on Leith Hill, 1890s. Image: Dorking Museum

Town Life

With a population of over 7,000 by the late 19th century, Dorking and the villages were home to civic institutions of all kinds: churches, chapels, schools, volunteer fire brigades, brass bands and benevolent institutions like the Oddfellows and the Ancient Order of Foresters.

At leisure the town hosted scores of clubs and societies: football, rugby and cricket teams, cycling and river swimming clubs; political societies, both supporting and opposing the vote for women; choirs, drama societies and bands. And no celebration, jubilee or coronation, was complete without sports, tea and a parade.

The Old Paulonians Cycling Club, George V coronation procession, 1911

The Dorking Fire Brigade at their fire station on West Street

Above: the Bury Hill Minstrels, 1895. Below: the boys of St Martin's church choir at Deepdene c1900

Above: Clarendon House, 1860s. Below: PJ Cook's, West Street 1911 All images: Dorking Museum

Howzat! The Cradle of Cricket

In the Long Room at Lord's cricket ground there hangs a painting of Dorking in 1770-80, showing a game of cricket in progress on Cotmandene.
This painting is one of the earliest known depictions of the game. The painting, by James Canter, shows the hills around the town dotted with mansions with the Deepdene, then home of Charles Howard 11th Duke of Norfolk, on the hill to the rear.
Cricket was born in Surrey, Sussex and Kent. The first recorded local game was at Mickleham Downs in 1730. By the 1760s it was well established on the Cotmandene (though the players depicted probably used only two stumps and a curved bat and may be using only one wicket). The pitch measured one chain in length (as today) but an over would last four balls and a match would usually be completed in one day. The row of tents along the side of Cotmandene provided refreshments to the spectators and gamblers who financed such matches.

The gentlemen of Coldharbour Cricket Club c1905. In 1845 a new ground on Mr Hope's land at Betchworth became home to Dorking's gentlemen players; the lower orders continued to play on the heavily sloping Cotmandene. Finally a suitable ground was established at Pixham, then remote from the town, at the instigation of Sir Trevor Lawrence of Burford Lodge in 1878. Cricket has been played there ever since. Image: Dorking Museum

Legendary professional cricketer Henry 'the Pocket Hercules' Jupp (1841-1889) was born on Cotmandene. He played for Dorking Balmoral club before being called up to play for Surrey, (for whom he played for 20 seasons), in 1859. With his partner, Tom Humphrey (1838-1878), from Mitcham, Jupp scored an opening 100 four times in their first season, at a time when Surrey County Cricket Club was the best in England. 'The Surrey Boys' both retired to Dorking: Jupp ran the Sun Inn and Humphrey moved to Westcott, managing the Ram Inn and then the Jolly Butchers.

A GRAND

Match of Cricket,

WILL BE PLAYED

At Lower Mitcham Green,

Between TEN GENTLEMEN of MITCHAM,

With WILLIAM DYER ESQ. of Blackheath.

AGAINST

TEN GENTLEMAN of DORKING,

With Mr. JUPP, of Reigate,

For One Hundred Guineas a Side,

On Monday the 26th of July 1819

Wickets to be Pitched at Nine o'Clock, and begin precisely at Half-past.

Mitcham,	Dorking,
Wm. Dyer Esq. G. M.	Mr. Jupp, G. M.
Mr. J. Chesterman,	Mr. S. Bothwell,
Mr. J. Sherman,	Mr. J. Bothwell,
Mr. Jas. Sherman,	Mr. Abel,
Mr. J. Bowyer,	Mr. Wren,
Mr. J. Gunnell,	Mr. Harman,
Mr. J. Bailey,	Mr. Phillps,
Mr. Jas. Rutter,	Mr. Fuller,
Mr. J. Wain,	Mr. Turner,
Mr. J. Merritt,	Mr. Peters,
Mr. J. Kingshot,	Mr. Blucher,
Mr. E. Chilman,	Mr. Boorer,
Mr. F. Crib.	Mr. Wells.

A Good Ordinary at the King's Head at Two o'Clock,

Flyer for a match of 1819 against Mitcham captained by Mr Jupp, father of local cricketing hero Henry Jupp. By the 1850s Dorking was one of Surrey's eminent clubs and Dorking gentlemen were instrumental in the founding of Surrey County Cricket Club.

Shrove Tuesday Football

The pre-match procession of Taffer Bolts Band - with drums, pipes and a triangle – in grotesque dress and with blackened faces in 1885. They were led by a man carrying the frame to which three footballs were attached. One ball was painted red and green, one red, white and blue, and the third in gold leaf. On the bar read the inscription: *'Kick away both Whig and Tory/Wind and water Dorking's glory'*. Image: Dorking Museum

Dorking's street football probably had its origins in the Catholic Lenten festivals that took place all over England before the Reformation.

On the morning of Shrove Tuesday shopkeepers barricaded their premises and children were given the day off school. Before the game a collection was made to pay for the ensuing damage. Then those who lived to the east of town took on their 'Westender' rivals.
At 2pm the game kicked off at the gates to St Martin's. Large numbers participated in play along the streets and over the Pippbrook until 6pm. Drinking and dinner at the Sun followed.

The game in play in the High Street. The game was long and play was rough. Damage to shop premises was not unusual. Image: Dorking Museum

The end came in 1897. Traders complained of lost trade, riotous behaviour and damage, and petitioned for its abolition. Though the District Council was in favour of the game, the County Council banned it. Extra police were drafted in as local people gathered to defy the authorities and a crowd of 2,000 watched as a Dorking councillor kicked off. Several balls were put into play to confuse the police, who managed to carry off 8 balls in attempts to stop the game. 52 people were fined for participating; in 1898 60 people, including the councillor who had kicked the game off, received fines.
But the authorities grew more effective in preventing any meaningful play and in 1907 the local paper declared the game extinct.

The football crowd in South Street in 1897. Image: Dorking Museum

Early Cycling in Dorking

Lewis Saubergue (right) and companions in 1870. Saubergue was one of the first locals to buy a velocipede in 1868. Saubergue's ironmongery workshop was situated on the site of Sainsbury's. In 1870 he and three companions went on a cycling tour of Germany on the newly invented 'penny-farthings'. Image: Dorking Museum

In 1875 Stanley Boorer, a delivery boy for Fuller's, cycled his clanking velocipede or 'bone shaker' from Denbies to Dorking after delivering a repaired sewing machine.

In the dark, with glow worms attached to his hat, he frightened the returning housemaids. But soon the sight was a common one.

In the 1890s Dorking's cyclists' camps were well known, their activities covered by the national press. Hundreds of cyclists from clubs from all over the south-east camped for 2 weeks at Poultry Farm, south of St Paul's school. Each club had a marquee as well as bell sleeping tents. Other tents housed local barbers, machine repairers, a post office and refreshments. In August 1896 over 6,000 people visited the camp, the highlight of which was a torchlight procession of cyclists in fancy dress through the town, lead by the town band.

Cycling gave women independence. Margaret Pennington, a campaigner for women's rights who lived at Broome Hall near Coldharbour, hailed the bicycle as 'nothing short of a social revolution'. But not all were in favour; in 1898 the landlord of the White Horse on the High Street made the national papers when he refused to admit a female cyclist in 'bloomers'.

Dorking Cycling Club at Mr Attlee's house on Rose Hill in the 1880s.The club was formed in 1887 and members were so appreciative of the council's road maintenance team that in 1896 they entertained 30 of them to supper. Image: Dorking Museum

A cycle party outside the Queen's Head. Not all inns were welcoming to cyclists: in 1899 the Burford Bridge Hotel attempted to charge Capel Cycling Club for each cycle left outside. Image: Dorking Museum

Right: Fuller's cycle workshop opened in 1892, selling and renting bicycles and giving cycling lessons. Image: Dorking Museum

DORKING CYCLING CLUB.

FIRST ANNUAL AMATEUR

ATHLETIC ✸ SPORTS

(Under N.C.U. Rules and A.A.A. Laws,) will be held

On WEDNESDAY, SEPT. 5th, 1888,

IN THE

CRICKET FIELD, PIXHOLME LANE, DORKING.

COMMITTEE.
MR. G. S. MATHEWS,

MR. F. A BEAUMONT,   MR. G. O. GODDARD,
„ E. R. BUTCHER,   „ W. RAPLEY,
„ A. J. FULLER,   „ H. WEBB.

Judges.—MR. ARTHUR FULLER and MR. E. L. TROWER.   Referee.—MR. J. A. WHITE.
Handicappers.—MR. C. MEAD, (Cycling Events.)   The EXECUTIVE COMMITTEE, (Athletic Events.)
Starter.—MR. A. J. FULLER.

A PROCESSION From Head Quarters, Bull's Head Inn, with the DORKING TOWN BAND,

AT 2 P.M.
The Sports commence at 3 p.m. precisely.   Open Events 4 p.m.

✤ PROGRAMME. ✤
OPEN EVENTS.

100-yards Handicap,	· ·	3 prizes of the value of	£2	£1	10s.	
One Mile Handicap,	· ·	3 „ „	£2	£1	10s.	ENTRY FEE,
One Mile Bicycle Handicap,	·	2 „ „	£2	£1		
Three Mile Bicycle Handicap	·	2 „ „	£2	£1		2s.
High Jump,	· · · ·	2 „ „	£1	10s.		
Long Jump	· · · · ·	2 „ „	£1	10s.		

CLOSED EVENTS.   Residents of the Parish of Dorking only.

120-yards Hurdle Handicap	·	3 prizes of the value of	£1	10s.	5s.		
100-yards Handicap, (Boys under 12)	3 „ „		10s.	5s.	2s. 6d.	ENTRY FEE,	
(1st Prize presented by MR. W. SELLMAN.)							
100-yds. Veteran Handicap (over 35 yrs.)	3 „ „		£1	10s.	5s.		1s.
220-yards Menagerie Handicap	·	3 „ „	10s.	5s.	2s. 6d.		
50-yards Sack Race	· · ·	3 „ „	15s.	10s.	5s.	Boys Race, 6d.	

EVENTS OPEN to Members of the DORKING CYCLING CLUB ONLY.

100-yards Handicap	· ·	3 prizes of the value of	£1	10s.	5s.	
One Mile Bicycle Handicap	·	3 „ „	£1	10s.	5s.	ENTRY FEE,
One Mile Tricycle Handicap	·	2 „ „	£2	£1		
(1st Prize presented by MR. G. O. GODDARD.)						1s.
Three Mile Bicycle Handicap	·	3 „ „	£3 3s.	£1 1s.	10s. 6.	
1st Prize presented by SIR TREVOR LAWRENCE, BART., M.P. 3rd Prize by MR. F. USHERWOOD.						

The Prizes will be distributed at 7 p.m. by LADY LAWRENCE.

All Entries with the Competitor's Club & Colours for the Races to be made to the Hon. Secretaries, on or before WEDNESDAY, AUGUST 29th.
HON. SECS.—S. W. FULLER, South Street.   JNO. WOOD, 43, Howard Road.

ENTRANCE SIXPENCE.   ENCLOSURE EXTRA. Tickets to be obtained of the above Committee or at the Gate.

C. ROWE, Machine Printer, 70½, South Street, Dorking.

Poster for the sports day of Dorking Cycling Club, 1888. The town band was in attendance, as at all town gatherings, and the prizes were to be given out by Lady Lawrence of Burford Lodge. Image: Dorking Museum

The Rise of the Car

On 27th November 1896 a car drove through Dorking for the first time.
By 1904 200 cars were passing through on summer Sundays and the council was spraying water on the unpaved road surfaces to dampen the dust stirred up. By the 1920s traffic congestion through the town toward the open spaces of the Holmwood, the Sussex Downs and the coast was intolerable.

The 1930s Dorking bypass (now the A24) was one of the earliest in the country. Despite much opposition the county council chose the cheapest route south, cutting through the grounds of the Deepdene close to its grand frontage. This made it far less attractive as a grand home. Its land attracted speculative builders and it began to be broken up for housing.

As demand for housing grew the beauty spots that surrounded the town were vulnerable to development. A large part of Box Hill was purchased by the financier Sir Leopold Salomons of Norbury Park and given to the National Trust in 1914 to protect it from development. Parts of Leith Hill were bought and donated to the National Trust by Cuthbert Heath of Anstie Grange. Holmwood Common was sold by the Duke of Norfolk to the county and local councils who gave it to the National Trust in 1955.

One of Dorking's first cars, a Benz owned by Mr Fuller of South Street, 1899.

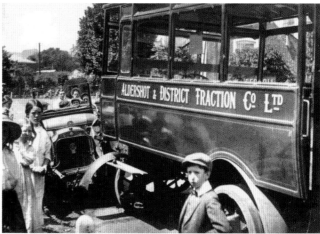

A traction engine accident on Coast Hill, Westcott 1905

Wescott's first motorized traffic accident, 1914

Left: The Dorking by-pass (A24) cuts through the Deepdene's parkland, paving the way for residential expansion as the estate was broken up, 1931-4.
All images: Dorking Museum

63

George Meredith

The poet and novelist George Meredith lived at Flint Cottage on the slopes of Box Hill.
He came across Mickleham on a walking trip and married local girl Marie Vulliamy at St Michael's in 1864. He wrote in a two-room chalet in the garden, often sleeping and eating there.

Meredith's work was radical, particularly in its treatment of women. *Modern Love* (1862) has been called the first 'modern' poem. *Diana of the Crossways* (1885), set at Crossways Farm in Abinger, fictionalises the struggle of Caroline Norton (grand-daughter of playwright Richard Brinsley Sheridan of Polesden Lacey) for a settlement on the breakdown of her marriage. In his old age he became known for his support for the vote for women and amongst his local circle were pioneering female foreign correspondent Flora Shaw of Little Parkhurst in Abinger and the suffragette Brackenbury women of Peaslake. He corresponded with the Leith Hill and District Women's Suffrage Society and wrote to The Times in support of Holmwood suffragette Emmeline Pethick-Lawrence when she was imprisoned in 1906.

Meredith celebrated the Box Hill countryside in verse and used it as a backdrop to his fiction. When no longer able to walk the hill he was pulled in a bath chair by a donkey called Picnic. Because of his religious unorthodoxy Meredith was denied burial at Westminster Abbey. He is buried in Dorking cemetery.

Flint Cottage was visited by Thomas Hardy, Algernon Swinburne, Robert Louis Stevenson, Oscar Wilde, George Bernard Shaw, George Gissing, James Barrie and HG Wells. When the cottage was full visitors stayed at the Burford Bridge Hotel which hosted a dinner in the writer's honour in 1895 attended by 40 leading writers.

Autograph hunters pursued the London literati who turned out for Meredith's funeral (left) at Dorking cemetery.

All the local women's suffrage organisations sent wreaths and tributes and good friend JM Barrie wrote an essay called *'Neither Dorking Nor the Abbey'*, imagining Meredith looking down on his coffin in amusement.

Crossways Farm, the setting for *Diana of the Crossways*, sits where Raikes Lane meets the A25 between Abinger Hammer and Wotton. It has a 17th century double porch. Painting by EW Waite

Laurence Olivier

Laurence Kerr Olivier was born at 26 Wathen Road, Dorking in 1907.

His father, Gerard Kerr Olivier, had abandoned a church career and married Agnes Crookenden whilst teaching at Boxgrove School in Guildford. The couple set up the Tower House School in Dorking in 1898. In 1903 Gerard was ordained into the Church of England. Appointed curate at St Martin's, he closed the school and the family moved to Wathen Road.

DORKING.—ON THE HILLS, 400 ft. above sea-level ; sandy soil, bracing air. A PREPARATORY SCHOOL for the Entrance and Scholarship Examinations at the Public Schools and for the Royal Navy. Reference is kindly permitted to the Head Masters of Winchester, Rugby, Uppingham, and late Principal of Cheltenham. Modern sanitation, large cricket field, gravel playground, workshop, gymnastic apparatus, drill, and swimming (during the summer). Prospectus on application.—Address, G. K. OLIVIER, M.A., The Tower House, Dorking.

Advert for Tower House School, Dorking. The 1901 census records that there were 8 pupils and 3 domestic staff.

The Dorking Swimming Club. Gerard Olivier is in the middle row, 5th from the left. He had a high diving stage erected on the Mole near the Club's bathing house close to Castle Mill. Previously bathers had had to climb a tree to dive. Rev Olivier also played cricket for Dorking.
Image: Dorking Museum

When Laurence was two years old, the family moved to a house named East Dene. In 1910 Reverend Olivier left Dorking for Notting Hill. Leaving many friends, he returned from time to time 'for refreshment and pleasure'.

Laurence Olivier's career on stage and film spanned more than six decades.
He directed and starred in *Henry V*, *Hamlet*, and *Richard III* and was instrumental in setting up the National Theatre. His awards included the Oscar for Best Actor, and Best Picture for the 1948 film *Hamlet*.

Though he never returned to live in Dorking, Laurence Olivier became patron of the Dorking Theatrical Society in the 1950s. In 1980 the Dorking and District Preservation Society arranged for a blue plaque to be placed on 26 Wathen Road commemorating his birth and brief residence in Dorking.

Left: Laurence Olivier's son Tarquin unveils the blue plaque at 26 Wathen Road.
Image: Dorking Museum

The Dorking and Holmwood Campaign

Above: the Mascot at South Holmwood, now the Dutch House. Image: Votes for Women by permisson of the British Library

Every weekend between 1906 and 1912 the leaders of the 'suffragette' campaign came down by train to Holmwood.

The Mascot (the Dutch House), home of social campaigner Emmeline Pethick-Lawrence (1867-1954) and her husband, Frederick (1871-1961), was the country home of Mrs Pankhurst's Women's Social and Political Union (WSPU). Women recovered there from forcible feeding and campaigns were planned there. In 1912 the house became the focus of anti-government protest.

Emmeline lead the WSPU with Mrs Pankhurst. She devised its purple, white and green colours; and, with Fred, she edited 'Votes for Women'. It was her fundraising and organisational skills and Fred's wealth that enabled the WSPU to make the impact that it did.

Mrs Pethick-Lawrence, standing, with Emmeline Pankhurst and Annie Kenney, with Holmwood driver, Mr Rapley, (who was famed for his discretion about WSPU matters), at the wheel. The Pankursts were frequently in Holmwood.

In 1912 the three were convicted of conspiracy to incite persons to commit malicious damage after a window smashing campaign. Fred and Emmeline were imprisoned and forcibly fed. When Fred refused to pay the costs of their prosecution the government put bailiffs into the Mascot and auctioned the contents.

For six weeks the WSPU conducted a campaign in Dorking and Holmwood to embarrass the government. They held rallies in Holmwood, Ockley, Westcott, Bookham and nightly in Dorking where organizer 'Charlie' Marsh assured worried tradesmen that there would be no window breaking spree. On 31st October 1912 3-4,000 people gathered for the auction of the contents of the Mascot, many coming down by train in suffragette colours. Most of the couple's possessions were bought back by supporters.

The Pethick-Lawrences spent the rest of their lives campaigning for freedom and equality, for the rights of women and the welfare of children. Entering parliament as a Labour MP after the First World War, Fred was created 1st Baron Lawrence of Peaslake in 1946. He negotiated Indian independence as Secretary of State for India in Attlee's government.

Mrs Pethick-Lawrence (right) marching at the head of a procession with Emmeline Pankhurst (middle). Christabel Pankhurst is behind (left). In 1913 women believed to be suffragettes carved 'V' and 'W' into the greens at the new Betchwoth golf course.
Image reproduced by permission of the Women's Library

Frederick William Pethick-Lawrence (1871-1961) by John Baker
'It is given to very few men to play a leading part in two great movements of emancipation' said Clement Attlee on the death of Frederick Pethick-Lawrence.
Fred played a major part in the campaign for women to be granted the vote, and in the granting of independence to India (which he had advocated for 30 years before becoming secretary of state for India in 1946. He was also a founder of the leading anti-war movement during the First World War, the Union of Democratic Control, while his wife, Emmeline, was treasurer of the Women's International League for Peace and Freedom. When conscripted at the age of 46 he refused to serve on the grounds that he was a political objector. Awarded an exemption as long as he did work of national importance, he went to work as a labourer at Wattlehurst Farm in Capel.
This painting was unveiled at Pethick-Lawrence House, the headquarters of the Dorking Labour Party, on 7th July 1962, by Lord Longford, during a day of commemoration for the lives of Fred and Emmeline. (Ex prime minister Clement Attlee had presided at the opening and naming ceremony for Pethick-Lawrence House in 1955). A portrait by the same artist of Fred and Emmeline hangs in Peaslake Village Hall. Image: Dorking Museum

Leith Hill Place

A branch of the Wedgwood family settled in the hills around Dorking in the early 19th century.

The innovative Josiah Wedgwood had made the family fortune with his pottery business in Staffordshire.

Caroline Wedgwood nee Darwin planted a rhododendron glade at Leith Hill Place. The establishment of gardens and parklands was typical of the incomers to the area who changed the landscape. On Caroline's death the house passed first to her daughter, Sophy, then to her daughter Margaret Vaughan Williams. Margaret's son, the composer Ralph Vaughan Williams, gave it to the National Trust in 1946. The National Trust's first tenants were Sir Ralph and Lady Wedgwood, whose grandson, Sir Martin Wedgwood (1933-2010) planned the donation of the Wedgwood Collection to Dorking Museum, including the piece pictured to the left. Image: Dorking Museum

In 1844 Josiah's grandson, also Josiah, moved to Leith Hill Place on the slopes of Leith Hill near Coldharbour. His wife Caroline was sister to the naturalist, Charles Darwin. His sister, Emma, was Darwin's wife. Darwin was a frequent visitor to Leith Hill Place. He conducted experiments into earth worm activity there, helped by his niece, Lucy Wedgwood, and at the nearby estate of Thomas Henry Farrer of Abinger Hall.

Alfred Russel Wallace

Charles Darwin.

In 1858 Alfred Russel Wallace, in a letter to Darwin, proposed natural selection as the mechanism underpinning evolution. This prompted Darwin into print with the theory on which he had been working for more than 20 years. Between 1876 and 1878 Wallace lived at what is now 12 Rose Hill in Dorking and although he proposed a meeting in Dorking Darwin's ill health prevented it.

By coincidence a noteworthy opponent of the theory of evolution, Bishop Samuel Wilberforce, son of the anti-slavery campaigner, was thrown from his horse and died at Abinger Roughs.

The cross marking the spot where Bishop Wilberforce fell in July 1873. Image: Dorking Museum

The Leith Hill Musical Festival

The Leith Hill Musical Competition was founded in 1904 by Margaret (Meggie) Vaughan Williams and Evangeline (Eva), Lady Farrer of Abinger Hall.

Eva presided and Meggie acted as secretary, cycling between Leith Hill Place and Abinger Hall. The first competition was held at Dorking Public Halls on 10th May 1905. Eight choirs from villages within a 10 mile radius of Abinger Hall competed in six classes: full chorus, male voices, female voices, madrigal, quarter and sight reading. The evening concert was conducted by Meggie's brother, Ralph Vaughan Williams, who, with other musicians, including Lucy Broadwood, chose the music.

It was always intended to hold the competition annually. (The only complete break was during the First World War). In 1908 Eva wrote that *'Dorking was worked up to an unknown pitch of excitement. Such a concert has never been in Dorking before. Hundreds were turned away from the door – but they stood outside and heard a good deal and joined loudly in the applause!'* Vaughan Williams attracted some of the most distinguished musicians of the day to participate. The composer, Gustav Holst, came in 1909 as an adjudicator and Hubert Parry presented the awards in 1911.

Ralph Vaughan Williams was devoted to the festival. He took village choir practices and inspired members to achieve difficult works. In 1931 Bach's St Matthew Passion was performed by a choir of 800 in the newly opened Dorking Halls. The Leith Hill Musical Competition contributed to the building fund for the halls. In 1950 the name was changed to the Leith Hill Musical Festival.

After Vaughan Williams' death in 1958 Dorking decided to honour his memory in bronze plaques at Dorking Halls and at St Martin's Church, and in its support for the Festival. In 2005 the Festival celebrated the centenary of this great community endeavour.

Top: The banner for the children's sight test event. All the participating choirs had their colourful embroidered banners. Middle: Miss Constance Travers with a festival banner at Rokefield, the Westcott home of choir organiser Mrs Carey Druce, 1905. Bottom: Westcott children's festival choir c1925
Images : Dorking Museum

Festival poster, 1929, designed by Joan Drew, an ex-campaigner in Dorking for women to be granted the vote. Her sister, Sylvia, conducted two festival choirs.

Ralph Vaughan Williams

'The composer must not shut himself up and think about art, he must live with his fellows and make his art an expression of the whole community.'

Ralph Vaughan Williams. Image: Dorking Museum

Ralph Vaughan Williams was the son of Margaret Wedgwood of Leith Hill Place and Arthur Vaughan Williams of Tanhurst. His grandmother was Caroline Wedgwood nee Darwin. When his father died, Ralph's mother returned to her family at Leith Hill Place. Growing up in his grandmother's house the young Ralph was encouraged in his first compositions by his aunt, Sophy Wedgwood.

After some time in London the composer returned to the area in 1928. From 1933 to 1953 he lived at the White Gates just off the Westcott road. He played a large part in the life of the town. He was a prime mover in the Dorking & District Refugee Committee, and provided the music for the Abinger Pageant to raise funds for Abinger church. (EM Forster wrote the text.) He tried out ideas for his 5th Symphony in another pageant, written for the Dorking & Leith Hill Preservation Society. All his life he worked for egalitarian ideals and with the Leith Hill Musical Competitions he fostered musical participation of the highest quality for the whole community, rich and poor.

Conducting the Abinger Pageant. Image: Dorking Museum

In the garden at the White Gates. Image: Dorking Museum

With neighbour Lucy Broadwood, Vaughan Williams was in the vanguard of efforts to preserve folk traditions. He recorded local gamekeepers and labourers, motivated by the chance of *'picking up some rare old ballad or an exquisitely beautiful melody, worthy, within its smaller compass, of a place beside the finest compositions of the greatest composers'*. Themes from traditional songs from all over the country (including Surrey) found their way into his own compositions.

Ralph Vaughan Williams remains a much loved composer. His 'Lark Ascending' (1920), suggested by a poem by George Meredith of nearby Box Hill, is frequently voted Britain's favourite piece of classical music.

EM Forster's Surrey Pageants

The novelist Edward Morgan Forster knew West Hackhurst, the Abinger home of his aunt Laura, from childhood.

Observation of her neighbours provided material for his descriptions of Edwardian Surrey's class hierarchies (*A Passage to India*, 1924), and stifling conformity (*A Room with a View,* 1908). He inherited the house and moved to Abinger with his mother in 1924. He was unsympathetic to the class distinctions of village life and at odds with the local gentry, who he felt had too much power.

Morgan (as he was known) had many friends nearby. Amongst them were Max Beerbohm in Abinger, birth control pioneer Marie Stopes at Norbury Park, and Labour MP Fred Pethick-Lawrence and his wife, Emmeline, in Peaslake. He played an active part in village life. In 1934 he wrote the *Abinger Pageant*, with Ralph Vaughan Williams providing the music, in aid of the church restoration fund. Four years later he wrote *England's Pleasant Land* for the Dorking and Leith Hill Preservation Society. He collaborated with Vaughan Williams to found the Dorking and District Refugee Society and when trying to sum up what was worth fighting for in the face of invasion during the Second World War, he wrote about Abinger and the lives of his neighbours.

Forster named his collected essays *Abinger Harvest*. When the lease on West Hackhurst ended in 1946 the villagers, who had initially found him aloof, if not distinctly odd, saw him off with a rousing party at which he gave a speech in defence of local footpaths.

Summer Street, in *A Room with a View*, is based on Holmbury St Mary. In the book the Rev Beebe is vicar of St Mary's (where Forster's aunt and mother are buried). Windy Corner, the Honeychurch family home, is set on the southern slope of Holmbury Hill and the skinny- dipping scene in a pond described as 'like swimming in salad' is probably based on the pond on the path to the hill.

Presented at Abinger Rectory, the Abinger Pageant had 500 participants including a band and a choir. Narrated by a woodman, it presented the history of Abinger, paying homage to John Evelyn for replanting trees lost to ironworking. Calling for the preservation of the countryside the woodman rails against arterial roads, bungalows, and pylons.

England's Pleasant Land, presented at Milton Court in 1938, compared 18th century enclosures, which robbed the peasantry of their common land, with 20th century death duties. The plot sees good Squire George's son forfeiting his land and Jerry the builder moving in chanting 'Ripe for Development is England's Pleasant Land'. There followed a pageant of horrors – cars, bikes, litter and pedestrians being run down. Image: Dorking Museum

The Battle of Dorking

The Battle of Dorking took place in 1875. Germany had defeated France and annexed Holland and Denmark. Britain declared war and Germany invaded an ill-prepared Britain. Troops came ashore at Worthing.

This fictional scenario was the basis for 'The Battle of Dorking', published anonymously in Blackwood's Magazine in 1871.

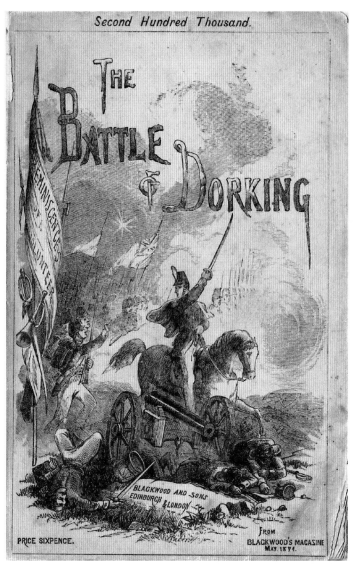

Written by Sir George Chesney, the plot sees the invaders engaged in battle at Dorking, strategically placed between the troops' landing point on the South Coast and London. Failure to defend the heights of Ranmore and Box Hill on each side of the Mole Gap allows the invaders to pass through to London. Britain is humiliated, its Empire lost.

The piece caught the public imagination. When reprinted it sold 80,000 copies and was translated into a score of languages worldwide. Military minds were soon exercised by the possibility of invasion through the Mole gap. There was no immediate response but in the 1880s forts were erected on Box Hill and Ranmore. And Lord Ashcombe, owner of Denbies, provided the local volunteer force with land and funds for a drill hall.

Though its notoriety arose from the concerns of its time, the birth of a unified Germany, the unfitness of the army, and the development of new means of transport and communication, the tale had a long life in public consciousness in both England and Germany. In the 1940s a German edition was issued to Hitler's army under the title *'Was England Erwartet'*, What England awaits.

Dorking's VCs

The Victoria Cross is Great Britain's highest military award for bravery. Dorking citizens are among those who have received this prestigious decoration.

Beresford and his son at Deepdene. When he died of peritonitis Lily gave £1000 to Dorking Cottage Hospital in his memory. Image: Dorking Museum

Sir William Leslie de la Poer Beresford VC

The son of an Irish Marquess, Beresford was nicknamed 'Fighting Bill'. He won the Victoria Cross at Ulundi in the Zulu war of 1879, rescuing a comrade whose horse had fallen on him by carrying the man to safety on the back of his own horse. When awarded the VC he insisted that the sergeant who had held the injured man upright also be decorated.

In later life Beresford lived at Deepdene with his wife, Lily, Dowager Duchess of Marlborough, and their young son. Beresford was Lily's third husband; she claimed to have married the first time (into the Vanderbilt family) for money, the second time (to the Duke of Marlborough) for a title, and the 3rd time for love.

Lance Corporal Charles Graham Robertson VC

Born in Yorkshire, Robertson came to Dorking as a boy when his father was employed as a gardener at Riverdale, Pixham. After attending St. Martins and Dorking High schools, Robertson joined the army and served in the Boer War. Robertson came to regard the Boer War as dishonourable and preferred to forget his part in it. A member of the Old Dorking Swimming Club, Robertson became a railway booking clerk and played football for Dorking.

Robertson again saw action when the First World War broke out. In April 1918, near Ypres, he halted a German advance until badly wounded in the stomach. For his valour, he was awarded the Victoria Cross. The town council was keen to honour Robertson but he refused any such adulation. He accepted a gold watch but asked that any other monies raised be put to charitable use. In December 1918 thousands turned out to watch him process by horse-drawn carriage to the Red Lion Hotel where the presentation was made. After the war Robertson returned to the railway. During the Second World War he was a sergeant in the Home Guard.

Roberton (centre) on the day of his presentation with a gold watch. Image: Dorking Advertiser

Dorking at War

When war was declared in August 1914 recruitment began immediately.

The town band accompanied the recruitment party from village to village. Farm workers were exempt from military service but other employers struggled to prevent their staff being called up.

The effects of war were immediately felt. Troops were billeted in town, horses were commandeered and bus services reduced. The surrounding woodlands were cut for pit-props and trench linings. Local Defence Committees compiled lists of horses, cattle and sheep, cars and motorcycles, and drew up plans to evacuate everything that might be of assistance to the Kaiser's armies.

It was a time of deprivation. Fuel was short and holly on the Holmwood was allocated for burning. Civilian organisations struggled. The voluntary fire brigades had to recruit from men over military age and older pupils undertook farm work. There were epidemics of measles, diphtheria and whooping cough.

The London Scottish Regiment kit inspection in Rothes Road, 1916. Image: Dorking Museum

Troops leaving Dorking on the Westcott Road, 1915. Image: Dorking Museum

Crowds watch as mobilised troops of 5th Batt, the Queen's Regiment (Dorking Company) board a train at Dorking station, 5th August 1914. The town band is playing on the platform. Image: Dorking Museum

ENROLMENT OF

SPECIAL CONSTABLES

COUNTY OF SURREY.

THE WAR.

It may be found necessary to enrol a certain number of Special Constables to do duty near their homes in the County of Surrey.

The Chief Constable of Surrey therefore requests that all loyal persons (not under 21 years of age) who may be willing to serve in the capacity of Special Constable, will give their names to the nearest Police Constable of the district in which they reside.

M. L. SANT, Capt.,

Chief Constable of Surrey.

GV RI

HE whom this scroll commemorates was numbered among those who, at the call of King and Country, left all that was dear to them, endured hardness, faced danger, and finally passed out of the sight of men by the path of duty and self-sacrifice, giving up their own lives that others might live in freedom. Let those who come after see to it that his name be not forgotten.

5750, RIFLEMAN, Joe STRUDWICK

8th Battalion.

Rifle Brigade (The Prince Consort's Own)

Killed in action, France & Flanders, 14/01/16

Born: Dorking, Surrey, Enlisted: Lambeth, Surrey, Residence: Croydon, Surrey

The town's youngest military casualty in the First World War was **Valentine Joe Strudwick** of Orchard Road. He was killed at the age of 15 years, 11 months - though his death certificate gives his age as 20, suggesting that he had lied about his age on joining up. Even younger was **Aubrey Hudson** of Newdigate who died on the Somme at just 15 years and 1 month.

The Anstie Grange Military Hospital

In October 1916 Cuthbert Heath offered his home at Anstie Grange between Holmwood and Coldharbour as a hospital for officers, fitting it out at his own expense.

Heath was an enthusiastic recruiter. He spoke at recruitment meetings in the villages and gave pep talks in his office at Anstie to men of Coldharbour and Holmwood who joined up. 'Our family is doing well,' recorded his daughter Genesta in late 1914. Seven of her eight male cousins had enlisted.

Cuthbert Heath was of a military family – the house was built by his father, Admiral Sir Leopold Heath, one brother was a general, another an admiral. Cuthbert had made his fortune in insurance. Responsible for transforming Lloyds of London from a specialist shipping insurer to the general world-wide insurer that it is today, he issued the first policies for burglary and motor insurance. During the war he advised the government on air raid insurance. Image by permission of JJ Heath-Caldwell

Casualties were brought by train from the coast to Holmwood station. Ambulances and lorries from Aldershot drove them to Anstie in convoy, often late at night. Stretcher bearers gathered in front of the house half an hour before the trains were due in. Then the Commandant, a nurse with a long white veil, a cloak and a lantern, would arrive in a car with huge headlights.
In February 1917 an unexpected patient arrived on one of these convoys, Cuthbert's nephew, Frederick Dunbar Heath. Frederick's parents, Arthur Raymond Heath and his wife, Flora, had been banned from Anstie but the ban was lifted to allow them to visit their son.
Nearly 700 patients passed through Anstie Grange.

Anstie Grange Military Hospital.

Left: Genesta Heath in 1914. Genesta worked as a pantry maid at the hospital. Right: The 26-bedroomed mansion was the setting for shooting parties, hunts and balls before the war, with 26 indoor staff plus gardeners, stablemen and chauffeurs. On the outbreak of war the indoor staff was cut to 3. Images by permission of JJ Heath-Caldwell

World War Two

War was declared on 3rd September 1939. Dorking businesses contributed significantly to the war effort.

Schermuly's Pistol Rocket Apparatus Company in Newdigate

produced maritime target identification flares and distress signals - rockets that sent up kites and aerials, cables attached to parachutes or that that could be used to illuminate water. The 55 acre site employed 1,400 people and trains, fifty or sixty wagons long, supplied the factory with gunpowder and explosives via Holmwood station.

Dorking foundry

worked day and night. Employing 60 people (including 13 women), it produced over 4,000 machine tools, 1,800 tons of iron castings and 300,000 screw-bomb nose-adaptors.

TO COMMEMORATE THE ADOPTION OF H·M·S· TITANIA BY THE CITIZENS OF DORKING WARSHIP WEEK MARCH ·1942·

Johnstons

produced gritters, sweepers and snowploughs. At least two Johnstons' snowploughs were in use by the Royal Air Force on each of over 600 airfields across Britain.

The Pneumatic Tent Company

made aircraft engine shelters for bombers and inflatable dinghies for aircraft.

After their working day local people served in the Home Guard, with Air Raid Patrols, the Civil Defence Volunteers, the Auxiliary Fire Service, the Women's Voluntary Service and the ARP Ambulance Service.

Stone & Turner's foundry shop in the High Street with tank traps stacked outside. Image: Dorking Museum

An Attlee's lorry collecting scrap aluminium for the Spitfire fund at the corner of Junction Road and West Street, 1940. Image: Dorking Museum

Canadian servicemen at the TocH club by Joan Warenne. The Dorking TocH services club was established in rooms over the milk bar at 116 High Street in May 1940. By July it was serving over 1,000 light meals a week to servicemen stationed locally. It had a games room with billiard tables and reading and writing rooms. Image: Dorking Museum

Evacuees and Refugees

The Dorking and District Refugee Committee

In 1938 the novelist EM Forster and the composer Ralph Vaughan Williams set up the Dorking and District Refugee Committee to help people fleeing Nazi Germany.

Refugees were housed at Clarendon House and at Fairhaven in Holmbury St Mary until the Duke of Newcastle offered Burchett House rent-free as a hostel. There the refugees received loans, medical assistance and help with finding work and housing. When war was declared in September 1939 Dorking's German nationals faced internment as enemy aliens and the Committee helped them apply to Home Office Tribunals to remain at liberty.

One of these was former women's magazine journalist Erika Schmidt-Landry whose writer husband was interned in the Isle of Man. Forster and Vaughan Williams took up her case when she was faced with putting her 3 small children into an orphanage.

The Dorking WVS with mobile canteen which provided sustenance to those coming into Dorking. The Dorking Congregational Church arranged lodgings with local families for Londoners bombed out of their homes. Image: Dorking Museum

Photographs of smiling evacuee children were published in the Telegraph and Daily Mail to reassure the public. Reports did not reveal the children's location, South Holmwood. '*I didn't know a holiday in the country could be so lovely. I shall always remember it,*' wrote one boy from Sydenham of his time there.

Above: The Dorking Nursery School, Junction Road. The nursery was set up by the Women's Voluntary Service in early October 1939 to provide a place for evacuee children to go during the day when many pre-school children, who were accompanied by their mothers, were required to leave their lodgings. Image: Dorking Museum

Evacuation to Dorking

3,000 children from South London arrived at Dorking station in September 1939. They were taken by bus to Dorking Halls where they were given a medical examination and a paper bag containing rations for 48 hours – condensed milk, tinned beef, biscuits and chocolate.

Local schools struggled to absorb the influx. Some worked double shifts, others took lessons outside. Some children from poorer areas were infested with lice: '*disgusting – you have my sympathy*' wrote the chairman of one school to the head. But the evacuees also had complaints: one girl was billeted with a woman of 80.

Wartime at Dorking's mansions

A train carrying Dunkirk survivors passes through Westcott, June 1940. Soldiers are holding out papers to communicate their survival to loved ones. Image: Dorking Museum

The Deepdene and Dunkirk

In 1939 the Southern Railway moved its headquarters from London to Deepdene.
A special train brought in many of its 800 workers daily and a complex of tunnels housed a telephone exchange, air raid shelters and an operations room from which the movement of evacuees, troops, supplies, munitions, ambulance trains and prisoners of war was organised.

In 1940 all normal railway traffic was suspended between 27th May and 4th June as 293 'Dynamo Specials', laden troop trains from the channel ports, passed through Dorking day and night carrying troops who had been evacuated from Dunkirk in France. Local people stood on stations and alongside the line to watch the trains with their cargo of men, some clothed only in blankets, pass. Notes thrown from carriage windows by desperate survivors were gathered up by passers-by and railway staff and posted on to loved ones.

Deepdene in1940, whilst occupied by the Southern Railway. Image: Dorking Museum

Denbies and the Home Guard school

During the Second World War Denbies became a training school for the southern Home Guard.
It was run by Major Hugh Pollock, husband of the children's writer, Enid Blyton, and the nearby chalk pits were used for bomb and explosives training.

Home Guard training demonstration at the Nower. Image: Dorking Museum

Bellasis House and SOE

Codenamed STS2, Bellasis House on Box Hill housed a training centre for Czech agents of the Special Operations Executive.
They were prepared there for their return under cover to occupied Czechoslovakia. The team that assassinated Reinhard Heydrich (the Nazi acting Protector of Bohemia and Moravia who had chaired the Wannsee Conference that set in motion the 'Final Solution'), set off from Bellasis for Prague in 1943.

Planes, Parachutes and Bombs

Dorking was not a military or industrial target during the Second World War but it suffered damage and casualties.

During the Battle of Britain, in the summer and autumn of 1940, planes fought in the skies above and several came down in the surrounding countryside. In the Blitz that followed German bombers often dumped unused bombs on the town and hills to lighten their loads on the return journey. And in the later days of the war flying bombs aimed at London caused indiscriminate damage.

All the local parishes were hit by bombs, rockets or incendiaries.

Miss Honorine Williamson in Dorking Air Raid Patrol uniform. Miss Williamson was brought up in Dorking, the niece of Vaughan Williams. She was killed when her home in London was bombed.

The South Holmwood Auxiliary Fire service with a car converted to carry a ladder.

Dorking Air Raid Patrol Ambulance Service, women ambulance drivers. All images: Dorking Museum

Miss Kathleen Spooner, fire watcher, from Hart Road, Dorking, with a stirrup pump.

German bomber down in Henfold Lane: 2 Dead plus 3 crew members
30th August 1940

The Heinkel drops its bombs whilst trying to outrun attacking Allied planes. A motorcyclist is severely injured and dies the next day. An elderly man dies whilst hurrying home to the Cotmandene Almshouses. Pigs are burned alive in their pen by a falling incendiary. Westcott Road, Sondes Place and Milton Court are damaged. The Heinkel then collides with an attacking Hurricane and crashes near Swires Farm, Henfold Lane, Holmwood. Three of the crew are killed; the pilot lands by parachute near Dorking. The Hurricane comes down nearby.

Bomb on Brockham: 5 dead
October 1940

Two houses in Nutwood Avenue destroyed killing a woman and her five-year-old daughter, a boy evacuee, and a woman and her two-year-old son. Other children are rescued from the rubble.

German bomber down at Holmwood: crew land by parachute
27th September 1940

People race to the scene when the pilot of the Junkers falls – badly burned and unconscious – by parachute in Yew Tree Road, Dorking. Other crew members land at Bradley Farm near Box Hill, Scammels Farm, Blackbrook, and the Norfolk Arms, Mid Holmwood. All are captured. A fifth crew member is killed when he falls from his parachute. The plane comes down at Folly Farm, Holmwood (causing a local woman

to miscarry), the gun turret at Pilgrim's Close, Westhumble, and the tail at Croft Avenue, Dorking.

One of the Germans who landed by parachute at Bradley Farm is escorted away.
Below: the army with a captured German airman's parachute.

82

Allied plane down in Westcott: a happy ending
22nd October 1940

A Hurricane is shot down and lands on a railway bank near Westcott. The Canadian pilot P/O Milne is taken to hospital in Dorking where he meets nurse Nan Jones who he goes on to marry.

Staff nurse Nan Jones who married Canadian pilot P/O JA Milne after meeting him at Dorking Hospital.

Bomb on Dorking: 3 dead
November 1940

Two houses destroyed in Fraser Gardens, Dorking, killing two sisters aged 12 and 20 when their home collapses. Their parents and two brothers survive, one brother being blown out of bed. A next door neighbour is also killed.

German bomber down in Ockley: 4 crew dead
March 1941

A night bomber is brought down in flames. Three crew members die in the plane, another is found dead in his parachute and the fifth is captured.

Boy killed 'souvenir' hunting
October 1942

A boy on a day trip from Brixton is killed and two others injured when they go looking for 'souvenirs' in the Dorking chalk pits where the Home Guard have been training. Elsie King, who lived near by, volunteers towels and linen for first aid, and is issued with extra coupons to replace them.

German bomber down in Capel
January 1943

The pilot of the Focke-Wolfe, realising that it is about to explode, warns approaching villagers to crouch. He gives himself up to two local brothers who had served in France in the First World War and are able to converse with him in French.

Bomb hits Westcott: 9 killed
January 1944

4 houses at Watson Road Westcott are destroyed, killing a woman of 92, two babies and two evacuee boys who were thrown from their bed, which landed on top of them.

German bomber down in Westcott: 2 crew dead
24th February 1944

The Dornier is shot down and crashes in Parsonage Lane. Two of the crew land by parachute at Wotton. Georg Trunsberger and Julius Schurgers are arrested by a special constable and taken to the Wotton Hatch Hotel.

The wreckage of the Dornier at Parsonage Lane.

Trunsberger and Schurgers receiving the Iron Cross before the mission which saw them taken prisoner in Wotton.

German bomber down in Holmwood: 4 crew dead
14th March 1944

The Junkers Ju88 is shot down by a British Mosquito whilst returning from a bombing raid on London and crashes on Holmwood Common near Blackbook. All the crew are killed on impact and locals report body parts in the nearby trees.

Pilot Straube who died at Blackbrook.

House hit in Sandy Lane: 2 killed
26th June 1944

Elm Cottage in Sandy Lane is destroyed by a flying bomb, killing two women and a boy. A few days later 74 year-old Elizabeth Cheeseman dies of shock when a flying bomb lands close to her in Ockley.

Abinger Church hit
3rd August 1944

Abinger Church is destroyed by a flying bomb just before the morning service is about to begin. The nearby Abinger Hatch inn, and Max Beerbohm's Manor House Cottage, are damaged.

Bombing raids and rocket attacks cease as the Allied armies advance through France and northern Germany, putting southern Britain out of the range of German bombers and un-manned rockets. At Dorking Urban District Council an incident map is prepared before the end of the war, showing all planes, bombs, and parachutists to have fallen on the area.

John Langdon-Davies

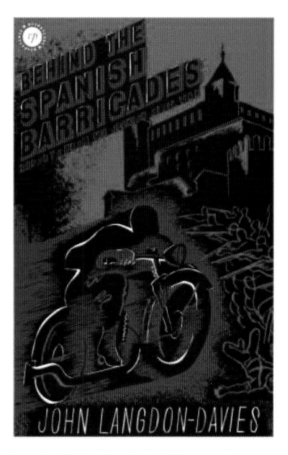

- from the Spanish Civil War to the Home Guard

John Langdon Davies, who lived at the Sundial in South Holmwood just outside Dorking was a prolific political writer.
He created the Jackdaw series of histories for children and wrote on Spain, science and history.

A conscientious objector and peace campaigner in the First World War, he spent much time in Spain in the 1920s, forming a bond with Catalan left-wing intellectuals.
Langdon-Davies covered the Spanish Civil War as a journalist and witnessed huge numbers of refugee children passing through Santander, one of whom had a note pinned to him saying: *'This is Jose. I am his father. When Santander falls I shall be shot, whoever finds my son, take care of him for me.'*
In response Davies founded the charity Foster Parents Plan for Children in Spain. Now known as PLAN the charity works in 45 countries.

During the Second World War Tom Winteringham (ex-commander of the British volunteers in the fight for democracy in Spain, who taught warfare techniques at the Home Guard school at Denbies), recruited Langdon-Davies into the command of the Home Guard. Making use of his battle experience, he became commander of the South Eastern Command Fieldcraft School. He wrote the 'Home Guard Fieldcraft Manual' and 'Home Guard Warfare' which were issued to all Home Guard units nationwide. After the war he was awarded the MBE.

Langdon-Davies' book about his experiences during the Spanish Civil War, Behind the Spanish Barricades. On his return to Spain to cover the war in 1936 Langdon-Davies travelled by motorbike, accompanied by his 16 year-old son.

John Langdon Davies in Spain in the 1950s with his two young sons by his second wife. Photo by permission of Patricia Langdon-Davies

Captain Pinkney and the Malta Convoys

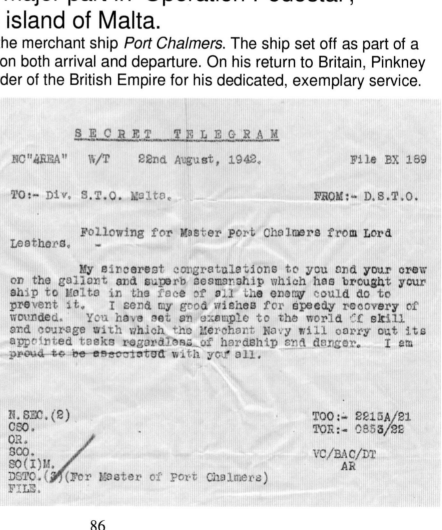

Captain Henry George Bacon Pinkney DSO MBE, a merchant navy officer, lived at Sunnyside near Blackbrook. In 1941 and 1942 Pinkney played a major part in 'Operation Pedestal', supplying the besieged island of Malta.

In July 1941 he was first officer of the merchant ship *Port Chalmers*. The ship set off as part of a convoy to Malta and was attacked on both arrival and departure. On his return to Britain, Pinkney was appointed a Member of the Order of the British Empire for his dedicated, exemplary service.

A year later he took command of the ship and set off again in a convoy of fourteen ships with a battleship escort. Though bombed south of Sicily, the Port Chalmers was one of only five merchantmen to reach its destination and the only one to do so without suffering damage or casualties. Pinkney was congratulated by secret telegram on the 'gallant and superb seamanship' which had brought his ship to Malta 'in the face of all the enemy could do to prevent it'. In recognition of his cool-headed skill and leadership, Pinkney received the Distinguished Service Order.

Images: Dorking Museum

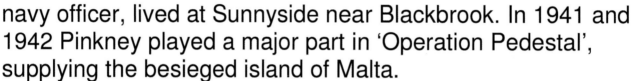

```
        SECRET   TELEGRAM

NC"AREA"   W/T    22nd August, 1942.           File BX 189

TO:- Div. S.T.O. Malta.                    FROM:- D.S.T.O.

            Following for Master Port Chalmers from Lord
    Leathers.

            My sincerest congratulations to you and your crew
    on the gallant and superb seamanship which has brought your
    ship to Malta in the face of all the enemy could do to
    prevent it.   I send my good wishes for speedy recovery of
    wounded.   You have set an example to the world of skill
    and courage with which the Merchant Navy will carry out its
    appointed tasks regardless of hardship and danger.   I am
    proud to be associated with you all.


N.SEC.(2)                                     TOO:- 2215A/21
CSO.                                          TOR:- 0853/22
OR.
SCO.                                          VC/BAC/DT
SO(I)M.                                         AR
DSTO.(3)(For Master of Port Chalmers)
FILE.
```

Tinker, Tailor, Actor, Spy

In 1943 a plane carrying the actor Leslie Howard (1893-1943) was shot down by the Luftwaffe en route from Lisbon to London with the loss of all passengers.

A commercial flight from a neutral country, it should not have been a military target. But there has been much speculation that Howard, officially lecturing for the British Council, was working for British intelligence in neutral Lisbon – a hotspot for the exchange of information between the warring powers – and that his plane was deliberately targeted.

Born in London of a Hungarian father, Howard bought Stowe Maries in Wescott in 1930 to provide an English home for his family. He and his family spent much of their time away from Hollywood at Stowe Maries, where he entertained many of his Hollywood friends in the private cinema in the garden.

Howard is best known for his role as Ashley Wilkes in *Gone with the Wind* which was released in 1939. When war broke out later that year Howard immediately returned to England to do his bit for the war effort.

Top: Howard in military uniform; Below: Howard's son Ronald (centre) playing cricket for Westcott against the Barclay & Perkins brewery team in 1938. The Barclays owned Westcott's Bury Hill estate whilst Augustus Perkins lived at Brookwood in neighbouring Holmwood. Left: the Howard family in the garden at Stowe Maries. Images: Dorking Museum

Brockham Park

and the birth of semi-synthetic Penicillins

The semi-synthetic penicillins developed at Brockham Park have had a huge impact on the fight against bacterial infection. Today they are used around the world in the treatment of infections in humans and animals.

The mansion at Brockham Park in Betchworth was purchased by the Beecham Group in 1945 and the Beecham Research Laboratories were opened there by Sir Alexander Fleming, the discoverer of penicillin, in 1947. The indoor riding school was converted into a chemical pilot plant and the stables into development labs. Wartime huts became the staff canteen.

The mansion at Brockham Park was built in 1882 as a private residence. In the new lab buildings in the grounds clavulanic acid was discovered, an enzyme inhibitor which stops the breakdown of penicillins by enzymes made by resistant bacteria. Images reproduced by permission of GlaxoSmithKline

Early research at the site concentrated on efforts to improve Beecham's food, toiletry and pharmaceutical product range. But by the 1950s the company had moved into the field of prescription medicines and was concentrating on the development of improved antibacterial agents.
In 1957 research carried out at Brockham Park led to the discovery of 6-aminopenicillanic acid (6-APA, the nucleus of the penicillin molecule).

The isolation of 6-APA chemical modification allowed new types of penicillin to be synthesised. Research and evaluation of the properties of these substances in the 1960s and 70s led to the birth of highly effective 'semi-synthetic' penicillins such as cloxacillin (used for staphylococcal infections) and amoxycillin (used for a range of bacterial infections). Countless people around the world owe their lives and health to the work carried out at Brockham Park.